I0555191

Moving in Place:

More Than Boxes— Moving Is About You (Not Just the Stuff)

By Jevata Crawford

Copyright ©2025 Jevata Crawford
ISBN 978-1-957863-46-7

All rights reserved. This book is independently published by the author. No part of this publication may be reproduced, distributed, or transmitted in any form or by any means, including photocopying, recording, or other electronic or mechanical methods, without the prior written permission of the author, except in the case of brief quotations used in reviews or critical articles.

For permission requests, contact the author at:
Project MOVE Press
Lehigh Valley, Pennsylvania

Credits
Cover Photography: Joan Zachary

Printed in the United States of America

First Edition, 2025

Dedication

To Dan, my partner and best friend—
You let me dream, find my path, and
shape my own style.
You welcomed every project I brought home
and every concept I had to try.
You are my quiet strength, my best choice—
and always the first thing I'd pack.

To my mother—
Thank you for carrying the boxes,
and for reminding me not to make them too heavy.

Acknowledgments

To my past, present, and future clients:

Thank you for trusting me inside your homes, your transitions, and your hearts. You let me test this method before it had a name. Your stories, your courage, and your willingness to move — physically and emotionally — gave shape to this work. Because of you, I found the clarity and confidence to make my own moves. This book would not exist without the people who moved with me — physically, emotionally, and creatively.

To my beta readers:

Thank you for your thoughtful feedback, your encouragement, and your willingness to sit with early drafts and raw ideas. You helped shape not just the pages, but the confidence behind them.

To everyone who listened, held space, and let me process aloud:

You know who you are. Whether it was over text, over dinner, or in the middle of a workday, thank you for reminding me I wasn't alone in this.

To the people who asked, "How's the book coming?":

You probably had no idea how much that question meant. Thank you for seeing me and this vision, even before it was fully formed. Thank you for your patience, your presence, and your grace when I needed it most.

And to the version of myself who kept showing up:

I'm proud of you. You did this with clarity, with care, a vision journal and with a whole lot of Post-it notes.

Table of Contents

Preface

Before we begin, I want to pause and say something important:

You made it here.

That might sound small, but it's not. You picked up a book about moving—which means something in you is shifting.

Maybe it's your space that no longer fits. Maybe it's your story that's ready to be rewritten.

Maybe it's your spirit saying, "It's time."

I wrote this book the way I speak—with space to think, breathe, and feel.

The rhythm of the words on these pages isn't what you'd expect.

That's intentional.

Sometimes the truth doesn't land in a perfect paragraph.

It lands in a pause.

In the room between sentences.

Because real moving happens in steps, not sprints.

And this book is meant to walk with you.

So take your time.

Reread the lines.

Underline what hits.

Rest when you need to.

And when you're ready...

Let's move.

Introduction

Moving in Place is not about rushing toward the next thing. It's about standing in the middle of your life—with all its complexity, beauty, and clutter—and choosing to move forward anyway. Not because everything is in order. Not because the timing is perfect. But because there's a version of you on the other side of this transition, who's waiting to be seen.

In these pages, I'll guide you through a process I've lived, shared, and shaped over the years—one that blends project planning with emotional clarity. I'll introduce you to Nia, a character whose move weaves together the stories of many people I've had the honor of walking alongside. Her story isn't linear or polished. But it's real, just like yours.

This is not a book about perfect moves. It's a book about honest ones—about creating a space where your grief can breathe, your hope can take root, and your next chapter can begin on purpose. You don't have to figure it all out right now. You don't even have to feel ready. You just have to keep turning the page.

We'll take this one box, one room, one breath at a time. And by the end, my hope is that you won't just feel more organized. You'll feel more at home in your own life.

Whether you're:

- relocating,
- downsizing,
- clearing out a loved one's home,
- supporting someone else through change, or
- quietly shifting something inside yourself—
  this book is here to meet you right where you are.

Hi, I'm Jevata. I'm a Move Manager.

This means I help people navigate the full experience of transition — not just the physical parts of a move, but the planning, decision-making, and emotional weight that comes with change.

Over the years, I've developed a clear, compassionate approach that blends structure with emotional insight. It's the same method I use with my clients, and it's the one I'll walk you through in this book.

The MOVING Method™

At the heart of this book is a flexible six-part approach I call the MOVING Method — a practical and emotional framework that helps you move with clarity, care, and purpose.

It's not about following perfect steps in order. It's about paying attention to what matters now, what needs to shift, and what will carry you forward.

You'll get to know it as you go. But for now, just know this:

How you move matters. And you don't have to do it alone.

What You'll Find Inside

There's a blend of story, structure, and support to help you make sense of your transition and take action in ways that feel honest, clear, and possible.

You may notice that some things are intentionally formatted a little differently — short lines, pauses, visual rhythm. That's on purpose. It's meant to mirror how transition feels: not always linear, but layered. A little messy, a little poetic, and deeply personal.

As you move through this book, you'll see these symbols guiding you. Each one marks a moment, a tool, or a truth to help you pause, plan, or take your next step.

📖 **Nia's Journey**—A moment that brings the concept to life.

✖ **MOVING Tools**—Offers practical frameworks, checklists, prompts, and templates you can put to use right away for clarity and momentum.

📦 **Unpack**—Creates space to reflect on what you're carrying—physically and emotionally—and what you're ready to release.

✍ **Journal With Me**—Invites deeper exploration through writing or quiet thought, helping you name what matters and what's next.

💬 *Moving Thought*—Shares short truths to keep as mantras and intentions—quick reminders to ground and guide you.

✪ **Jevata-isms**—Delivers small truths—nudges, whispers, and grounding breaths drawn from my own lived experience with moving and change.

You'll also find this key in the MOVING Toolkit for easy reference.

How to Use This Book

Use *Moving in Place* as a guide. Use it as a mirror. Highlight. Scribble. Pause. Return. This book walks with you—not ahead of you.

Here are a few ways to move through it:

- **Start where it makes sense.** You don't have to read in order. Follow your need—your move may not look like someone else's.

- **Build your Move Plan.** In Chapter 5 you will walk through each part, step by step. Chapter 4 shares Nia's Journey and her sample plan —a lived example to help you see how the process can begin, even before everything is figured out.

- **Explore the MOVING Toolkit.** In the back of the book, you'll find checklists, journaling prompts, decision-making frameworks, and templates—all designed to give you structure when you need it.

✗ TOOL 1: MOVING Method Tracker

This tool gives you a place to pause, notice and capture what's happening. Your answers may shift as you grow more familiar with your values and how they shape the way you move.

✪ Jevata-ism

You don't have to do it all at once.
You don't have to do it perfectly.
You just have to begin.

And the good news is:
You have a plan.
You have a process.
And you have a partner.

Let's begin.

CHAPTER 1:
A Beginning

Before anything moves, there's a moment. Not a list. Not a label. Just a quiet shift in your chest. You're still—but not settled. This isn't about organizing your closet. It's about organizing your courage. About making space for the life you're ready to live.

MOVING. A shift that begins before anything is packed. Moving begins with a feeling—a quiet knowing that something no longer fits. A nudge in your chest. A truth you haven't said out loud yet. Even if everything looks the same on the outside, something inside you has already started to move. Moving is an unraveling. A releasing. A reckoning with who you've been and who you're becoming. It's the moment you realize the clutter isn't just stuff—it's stories. The calendar isn't just busy—it's full of obligations that don't reflect your priorities. The space isn't just messy— it's misaligned.

IN. The quiet center of it all. The part we usually skip— but where transformation takes root. *In* is where the work happens. It's the pause. The presence. *In* means inside yourself. It means within your current life. It means being honest about what's real—before anything gets rearranged. *In* is not passive. It's powerful. To move in place is to be with what's uncomfortable long enough to understand it. To sit with the mess without judgment. To choose clarity before motion.

PLACE. The space you shape—and the one that shapes you. Place is layered. It's the physical space around you—but also the emotional space within you. Place isn't always about location. It's about alignment. It's not just where you live— it's how you live there. To own your place means to make peace with what's here—and shape it in service of what's next.

MOVING IN PLACE. When movement meets meaning—and place is both a location and an identity. It's not about waiting for the perfect time or rushing toward the next thing. It's about becoming honest about what needs to shift in order to transition—inside and out. Every move has a shape. Some are quiet. Some are chaotic. Some are about grief, others about growth. This book will name a few of those Move Types to help you see where you are—and what's possible next. It's awareness. It's intention. It's naming your next chapter with clarity, not chaos.

Moving is always about more than boxes. It's about story. It's about legacy. It's about becoming.

📦 Unpack: What Are You Really Moving?

Before the toolkit. Before the plan. Pause.

- What are you holding onto emotionally right now?

- What fears—or hopes—are already starting to surface?

- How do you want to feel at the end of this move?

You don't need to answer everything perfectly. Just start by being honest. Let this be your first moment of movement.

My First MOVE

Project MOVE didn't start with a brand or a business plan. It started with a question: How can I help?

For over a decade now, I've helped people through some of life's most overwhelming transitions—downsizing after retirement, clearing homes after loss, and navigating identity shifts after major change.

The very first move I managed wasn't for a client. It was for a friend — and, unknowingly, for myself.

At the time, I was buried in my own clutter — physical, emotional, and aspirational. I had just been downsized from a job that had become my identity. And when it ended, it felt like I did, too. The loss wasn't just professional — it was personal. I was standing in the middle of a life that no longer made sense, unsure how to move forward.

Then a friend called. She was merging households and overwhelmed by the logistics, emotions, and layers of starting again. She thought I could help her organize her things — but what she really needed was someone to help her make sense of what came next. To navigate the overlap of lives, identities, and needs. To bring order to a transition without losing what mattered most.

And somewhere in the process of helping her move forward, I realized: I was doing the same for myself.

And what I discovered was this: When I stepped into her overwhelm, I stepped out of my own. I didn't just help her move — I helped her move forward. And in doing so, I began to rebuild my own foundation.

That experience became the beginning of the work I now call Project MOVE.

From Experience to Framework

That first move lit a spark. But it wasn't a one-time moment — it was the beginning of something bigger. I started to see consistent patterns in the way people moved, the emotions they carried, and the breakthroughs they experienced when given the right kind of support.

I realized moving isn't just about boxes or labels. It's about managing change with intention — and reclaiming your space when life feels out of alignment.

My background helped. I've led teams, coordinated logistics, and held space for grief, indecision, and transformation. What began as a simple offer to help became the foundation for something much more intentional.

With every client I served, the framework started to take shape. I began noticing what people needed: not just structure, but compassion. Not just checklists, but clarity.

That's how the MOVING Method™ was born. It wasn't crafted in theory—it was shaped in living rooms, garages, basements, and closets. It's the method I use every day in my business, Project MOVE, to help real people navigate life's most emotional and practical transitions.

✍ Journal with Me

Before anything changes on the outside, take a moment to check in with what's shifting inside.

This is your chance to set the tone for your next chapter—not just in your space, but in your story.

- How do you want to feel in your next chapter?

- What are you ready to release or leave behind?

- What do you want to invite in?

- Complete this sentence: In this next chapter, I am becoming ...

Now, pull it all together in your own words. This is your Move Vision Statement—something you can return to whenever the process feels messy or hard.

🛠 TOOL 2: Move Type and Vision Statement Worksheet

This tool helps you define how you want to feel, what you're leaving behind, and the values that will guide your move forward.

Before anything changes on the outside, take a moment to check in with what's shifting inside.

There are many different kinds of moves—some filled with grief, some driven by growth. Some are physical, others are about reclaiming your space or stepping into a new version of yourself. In this tool, you'll begin by identifying what kind of move you're making. You'll see a few Move Types listed to help guide you—but there's always space to name your own.

This is your chance to set the tone for your next chapter—not just in your space, but in your story.

📖 Nia's Journey: Introduction

Nia is 53, recently single, and grieving the loss of her mother—whom she cared for in her final years. She now stands in the home she inherited, surrounded by love, memory, and the weight of what remains.

But Nia is more than one person. She is a composite of many lives, many stories. Her name—*Nia*, meaning "purpose" in Swahili—is not accidental. It's a quiet declaration that every move we make, especially the hardest ones, can be rooted in meaning.

She reflects the emotional truth of so many people I've walked alongside: caregivers, culture bearers, first-generation success stories, eldest daughters, memory keepers. People navigating the tension between legacy and liberation.

Nia's journey isn't linear or easy. But it's honest. Through her reflections, fears, and small brave steps, you'll see the MOVING Method in action—not as a concept, but as a lived, felt, sometimes messy process.

Think of her not as a single story, but as a companion. A mirror.
Not because her details match yours, but because her courage might remind you of your own.

💬 *Moving Thought*

Each move I've made—both physical and emotional—has asked me to be honest, to be brave, and to get clear.

That's where the MOVING Method began. Not in theory, but in my lived experience.

It started with questions: What if my space could hold more peace than pain?

What if I gave myself permission to evolve within the walls I already lived in?

I've witnessed the quiet magic of intentional moving—how clearing, organizing, and redefining a space becomes an act of reclaiming your identity.

Because when you move with intention, you don't just change your surroundings. You change your Self.

Project MOVE began with survival—and the deep desire to help others find their footing in seasons when nothing feels steady.

So let this be your reminder: Every transition is sacred. It's a chance to realign your space with your vision, your values, and your future self.

You're not just moving out. You're moving in.

CHAPTER 2:
Naming the Moves We Make

Every move tells a story—and every move has a type.

Some are loud and sudden. Others are quiet and long overdue. But before we can move forward, I want you to understand the types of moves and the story each one holds.

I want to invite you into the heart of what moving truly is—a personal shift that deserves to be named, understood, and honored. In this chapter, we'll explore the different types of moves people make, so you can see yours clearly.

In Chapter 1, we explored how *Moving in Place* is about more than packing—it's about clarity, intention, and becoming.

This chapter continues that conversation with two essential questions:
What is your move pattern? And how will you name it?

Your story.

Your starting point.

What follows is a reflection—a poetic roadmap that captures the many layers of this experience and sets the emotional tone for the practical work to come. Whether your move is joyful, complicated, long overdue, or completely unexpected, let these words meet you exactly where you are.

The Patterns of the Moves We Make

We move out,
from homes and habits,
from versions of ourselves
that no longer fit the frame.

We move in,
to new beginnings—
fresh walls, clean slates,
and rooms waiting to be claimed.

We move together,
with hands that lift,
with laughter echoing through
tape and torn-down lists.

We move apart,
when paths diverge—
love or loss,
or time's quiet urge.

We move up,
chasing ceilings turned to sky,
stepping into roles
that once passed us by.

We move forward,
even when feet drag—
pulled by hope,
or pushed by the past.

We move through,
storms and slow goodbyes,
grief wrapped in linens,
truth in tear-lined eyes.

We move with purpose,
not just to leave,
but to arrive —
to live with intent, to breathe.

We move with memories,
in every box, every fold —
in ticket stubs and
    photo frames,
in stories still untold.

And sometimes,
we stay —
but shift everything.
We reclaim rooms,
paint new colors,
and finally choose how
    we want to live.

And always —
we are moving in place.
Shaping the space we
    call our own,
carving a life that feels
    like home.

The poem you just read reflects the emotional truth behind moving—the quiet grief, the fresh hope, the tangled in-between.

Over time, I began to notice something: While every story is unique, there are certain rhythms that repeat.

Echoes in the emotions. Familiar threads in the questions. Patterns in the reasons people choose to move—or stay.

These patterns helped me support my clients more clearly. They gave structure to what often feels like chaos.

But none of that matters more than this:

Your move is your own.

And before you do anything else, I want to invite you to name it. Because naming your move is how you begin to move with intention.

📦 Unpack: Questions Before You Begin

As you reflect on what surfaced for you in the poem—whether it was a single line or the feeling of the whole—you might begin to notice what this move is really about for *you*.

Beneath the boxes and timelines, there's always something deeper: a need, a hope, a letting go.

That's why before we move into planning, I invite you to pause, to unpack—not your belongings, but your intentions.

- What's really driving this move? (Is it growth, healing, adventure, necessity, something else?)

- What do I hope to find or feel on the other side? (Peace? Freedom? A fresh start?)

- What part of myself am I bringing with me? (Strength, resilience, a new dream?)

- What part am I ready to leave behind? (Old fears, outdated expectations, burnout?)

- If I could name this move, what would I call it? ("The Big Leap," "Homecoming," "The Reset," "Finding Center" — or something all your own.)

There are no right or wrong answers. They don't even have to make sense to anyone but you.

This is your move — and naming it helps you claim it.

Write it down, whisper it to yourself, or just hold it quietly in your heart — but give this moment a name.

✗ TOOL 3: Name Your Move Worksheet

This tool helps you give your move a name that reflects its deeper meaning and emotional purpose.

💬 *Moving Thought*

When I first started noticing the patterns in how people move, I realized something big: The way I approached each transition held deeper truths about who I was and what I needed. That realization became one of the seeds of the MOVING Method—a way to bring clarity, self-awareness, and grace to every kind of shift, not just the ones that come with a change of address.

It's never just about a change in location. It's about identity.

It's about loss.

It's about hope.

And above all—it's about naming what this moment really is.

I once called a move "The Great Escape" because I needed to run from burnout and reclaim peace.

Another I labeled "The Second Start," because I was rebuilding everything from scratch after a job loss.

Naming my moves helped me give language to what felt overwhelming. It helped me hold space for both grief and possibility. And it gave me permission to move at my own pace.

This chapter's poem is my love letter to the many ways we transition—sometimes quietly, sometimes messily, always meaningfully.

I hope it reminds you that even if your move doesn't fit neatly into one box or one label, it is worthy of being named, honored, and seen.

CHAPTER 3:
Move Readiness

Before we make a plan, let's take a breath.

You've named your move. Congratulations. You've sat with what it means to be here — in this moment of shifting. Now it's time to check in with where you really are.

✂ TOOL 4: Move Readiness Check-In

This chapter introduces the Move Readiness Check-In — but don't think of it as a test. This isn't about how prepared you are on paper. It's about checking in with your mindset, your energy, and your willingness to be honest with yourself as you move forward.

It's about getting honest with yourself — emotionally, mentally, energetically. Because readiness isn't just about lists and logistics. It's about noticing what you're carrying and whether you're trying to drag it into the future.

This tool is here to help you reflect on your mindset, name your fears, and start to shape what moving forward actually looks like. No pressure. No right answers. Just a mirror, and a moment.

Move Readiness Check-In

Statement	Strongly Disagree 1	Disagree 2	Neutral 3	Agree 4	Strongly Agree 5
I understand why this move is necessary or meaningful right now.	O	O	O	O	O
I feel emotionally ready to make changes in my environment or routine.	O	O	O	O	O
I have a sense of what I want to feel or experience on the other side of this move.					
I have an idea of where or how to begin.	O	O	O	O	O
I have support—emotionally, practically, or spiritually—for this process.	O	O	O	O	O
I trust myself to make thoughtful decisions during this move.	O	O	O	O	O
I see this move as an opportunity to align more closely with my values.	O	O	O	O	O

Score Range	What It Might Mean
8–16: Rooted Reluctant	You might be feeling overwhelmed, but unclear or stuck. That doesn't mean you're not ready—it means this move deserves more time, support, and tenderness. Let Chapter 7 walk with you through fear, and use the MOVING Toolkit to ground yourself before making major decisions.
17–26: In the Middle of the Mess	You're not standing still—but you're not sure where it's all going yet. This is the most common place to be. Your move will require reflection, intention, and structure. Stay close to the MOVING Method and Move Plan, and give yourself permission to go one step at a time.
27–40: Ready to Begin (Even If It's Still Tender)	You're already in motion. You've named your "why," and now you're ready to plan with purpose. Your clarity is a powerful asset—build a Move Plan, using Chapter 5 that honors it, and keep your values close throughout the process.

No matter your score, **this isn't a test**—it's a check-in. Use this tool as a compass, not a judgment. The MOVING Method will meet you wherever you are and help you move from intention to action—with care, not chaos.

Toolkit Highlight—Move Readiness Check-In. This is the only tool printed in full inside the book, it's placed here because readiness isn't just a concept—it's your entry point. You'll also find this tool referenced in the Toolkit at the back of the book.

Unpack: Reflections on Readiness

- What surprised you about your responses?

- Where did you feel the most hesitation or tension?

- What kind of support—emotional, practical, or spiritual—might you need before taking your next step?

This isn't a test. It's a mirror. Uncertainty is allowed here. Awareness creates options. And options give you power. This is your pause before the plan—your first act of self-trust.

Moving Thought

Readiness isn't a feeling—it's a decision to be honest. You don't have to be fearless. You just have to be willing.

CHAPTER 4:
The MOVING Method — Nia's Move Plan

Now that you've paused to assess your readiness, you likely have a better sense of where you are — what feels clear, what feels heavy, and what still feels uncertain.

This is where intention meets structure.

In this chapter, you'll begin building your Move Plan — your personal roadmap for what's next. Not a rigid checklist, but a grounded, flexible framework rooted in your needs, your vision, and your pace.

So, What Is a Move Plan?

A Move Plan is your personal project plan
for navigating transition.
It brings together your vision, timeline, priorities, and support system — so you can stay focused, flexible, and clear as you move forward.

It's not just about what to do with the boxes.
It's about building a map that reflects your *why*, shows what needs to happen, and reminds you how you want your next chapter to feel.

I've managed dozens of moves. Before that,
I was a Project Manager.
I know the value of a solid plan.
Without structure, even the best intentions
get lost in the chaos.

A Move Plan helps you see the big picture, break it down into manageable parts, and move with purpose.

This isn't about perfection.
It's about making space for what matters — step by step.

Nia didn't feel ready. But she knew it was time.
So she wrote down what she could—a few truths, a few
hopes—and gave herself permission to begin.

That's what this chapter will help you do, too.

✖ TOOL 5: Move Plan Template

If you're ready, dive in.

You don't need to have it all figured out.
You just need a place to begin.

With a Move Plan, you make intentional progress—not just
check boxes.
You center what matters, instead of reacting to whatever's
shouting loudest in the moment.

This isn't just about staying organized.
It's about staying grounded.

Your Move Plan is your compass.
It turns the moving process into something manageable,
meaningful, and measurable.

It's a blueprint for the life you're building—one choice,
one room, one value at a time.

So when someone says, *"I'm moving,"* the next question
should always be:

"What's your plan?"

📦 Unpack: What's Getting in the Way of Planning?

- What emotions come up when you think about creating a plan?

- Do you feel pressure to "get it right?"

- What do you need—emotionally or practically— to begin?

- Can you give yourself permission to start without having all the answers?

Laying the Foundation—Nia's Move Plan

You don't have to do it all at once. But you do need a place to begin. This is it.

You remember Nia. She didn't start with certainty. She started with a pen, a little honesty, and permission to not get it all right.

Her plan is an example—not of perfection, but of motion. What matters is not how polished it is, but that it reflects her values, her vision, and her needs at this point in time.

Nia's role is to walk alongside you through this journey— not as an expert, but as someone figuring it out in real time, just like you.

What follows is her first attempt at building her Move Plan.

It's honest. It's in progress. And it's enough to get started.

This is the kind of clarity that comes from showing up—
not from having all the answers.

Use this as a guide, a spark of inspiration, or simply a
reminder, that where you are right now is the best place to be.

 Nia's Journey: Move Plan Starting Point
(Before discovering the MOVING Method™)

Move Name: *(blank)*

Project Summary:
I need to do something with the house. It still feels like
hers. I don't know if I'm staying here long term, but I can't
keep living like this. There's too much stuff. I feel stuck. I
just want to feel like I can breathe again.

Move Type: *Legacy Move*

Current Situation:
- My mom's things are everywhere
- I don't go into half the rooms
- I haven't touched her closet
- I feel guilty getting rid of anything
- I'm exhausted from work and don't know
  where to start
- It's just me

Goal of the Move:
I don't have a big, clear goal yet. Right now, I just want the
house to feel lighter. If I can walk into any room without
feeling like I'm intruding on what used to be life—that
would be enough."

Vision + Success Statement:
Vision? Honestly... I just want to feel like I live here. Maybe someday I'll have friends over. I miss that. *Success?* I guess it would feel like I'm not drowning in memories.

Timeline + Key Milestones:
- No set timeline, I want to be done already
- I want it to feel different by summer
- Maybe I'll sort the kitchen first?
- I keep avoiding it
- I don't know what counts as a milestone

People Involved + Roles:
- Gee said she'd help, but I haven't asked yet
- I don't want to bother Eva (she's busy)
- My therapist mentioned taking it one room at a time

Key Projects + Tasks:
- Go through clothes
- Do something with the papers in the dining room
- Try not to get overwhelmed
- Maybe list some furniture?
- Figure out what I want to keep
- Buy trash bags

Self-Care + Stress Management:
- Sometimes I light a candle before I start
- I skip whole weekends because I'm too tired
- I feel bad that I'm not doing more
- I try to go outside when I feel like crying
- I don't really have a system yet

✍ Journal with Me

Take a breath. This is your space. After reading Nia's Move Plan, you might be feeling a mix of things—hopeful, unsure, maybe even overwhelmed. That's okay.

Let this be your gentle beginning. You don't have to complete it all today—just start with what's true.

- What kind of move are you in right now—physical, emotional, or both?

- What do you already know about what you want or need?

- What's still unclear—but asking for your attention?

- Where do you feel resistance—and where do you feel ready?

💬 *Moving Thought*

A plan doesn't need to be perfect to be powerful. It just needs to begin—honestly, gently, and with room to grow.

That's where the MOVING Method comes in.

CHAPTER 5:
The MOVING Method™ —
A Framework to Move with Clarity, Purpose, and Peace

You may have started your Move Plan.

Maybe you've named your move, captured what you know or simply started.

Where ever you are — you are in the right place to begin.

Now, it's time to fill in the Move Plan — with intention.

The MOVING Method™ is more than a checklist.

It's a rhythm.

It meets you where you are and helps you move — emotionally, practically, and meaningfully.

This chapter is where that rhythm comes to life.

Each letter of MOVING offers something deeper than tasks. It gives you:

- A way to name what matters

- A way to stay grounded

- A way to move forward — even when you feel stuck

You'll see how this framework lives inside real stories, including Nia's.

You'll reflect on your own. And you'll find tools you can return to again and again — not just during this move, but anytime change comes knocking.

Whether you're carrying grief, making a fresh start, or reshaping your space to reflect who you are — this method holds it.

✖ TOOL 5: Move Plan template

Your core tool—the project plan that brings every section of your move together into one clear framework.

What is The MOVING Method™?

The MOVING Method is a practical, flexible framework for navigating any life transition — whether you're clearing a loved one's home, starting over, or reclaiming space for yourself. It offers both **emotional grounding** and **tactical structure**, helping you move forward with **clarity, presence, and self-trust**.

Each letter represents a core focus area that shows up in every kind of move. The method supports decision-making, organization, and momentum — without forcing a one-size-fits-all path.

This is your compass. It won't just tell you what to do — It will help you remember **why it matters**.

MOVING Method™ Framework Overview

Letter	Themes	Focus	Guiding Questions
M	Motivation, Mindset, Make Space	Name your move, map your why, and clear space—physically and emotionally—for what's next.	Why am I moving? What needs to shift or open?
O	Ownership, Organization, Order	Step into the lead, own your story, and structure the support you need.	What's real right now? What needs structure?
V	Vision, Values, Voice	Define what matters most—and let your next chapter reflect it clearly.	What do I want? What matters most?
I	Involvement, Intuition, Insight	Trust your gut, ask for help, and stay connected to your inner knowing.	Who's with me? What do I know deep down?
N	Navigation, Now, Next	Take it one step at a time. Set your course. Move from now to next with clarity.	What's the next right step?
G	Growth, Grace, Grounding	Reflect on your journey. Release what no longer fits. Carry forward only what honors who you're becoming.	How am I becoming? How do I reflect and stay rooted?

How to Use the MOVING Method™

Think of the MOVING Method as both a guide and a
conversation.
It blends planning with reflection—helping you move
forward with clarity, not confusion.

This is the same approach I use with clients:
Asking thoughtful questions.
Listening deeply.
Shaping their answers into a Move Plan rooted in purpose.

You don't have to do it all at once.
You can return to it whenever you need.
And you can trust that this method will hold you through
the process.

Here's how to begin:

1. Start with "M"—Motivation.
   Name your move, your why, and begin outlining your plan.

2. Follow the method as a guide.
   Each letter gives you questions and tools to help
   organize, decide, and move forward.
   You can go in order—or jump to what feels most urgent.

3. Use the Move Plan as your story map.
   As you reflect and make decisions, write them directly
   into your Move Plan.
   It becomes both a strategy and a snapshot of your journey.

4. Come back when you feel stuck.
   These prompts work like personal coaching tools—
   they're here to offer clarity when you feel overwhelmed.

5. Give yourself permission to go at your own pace.
   Moving isn't a race—your progress matters more than
   your speed.

6. Apply it to any kind of move.
    Whether you're packing a house, clearing an estate, or
    navigating a personal shift, this method supports it all.

7. Reset and revisit. Your move will evolve.
    Your answers might too. That's expected.
    This method is built to grow with you.

You'll learn how a Move Plan can hold more than just your
to-do list.
It can hold your hopes, your resistance, and your real-time
process.

Now it's time to fill it in — with clarity, care, and your whole
self in mind.

This framework isn't about checking every box perfectly.
It's about finding your way through a season of
change — with intention, reflection, and support.

Each letter — Motivation, Ownership, Vision, Involvement,
Next Steps, and Growth — invites you to reflect, decide, and
move with purpose.

Your move isn't a checklist.
It's a rhythm.

Some days, you'll lead with Vision.
Other days, you'll return to Mindset.

That's not going backward.
That's Moving in Place.

Each letter of the MOVING Method™ is explored through five parts:

1. **What this letter means**
   → Grounding definitions + purpose

2. 📖 **Nia's Journey** —
   A moment that brings the concept to life.

3. **Your Move Plan in Action**
   → Which sections of the Move Plan align with each letter + related tools
   → Toolkit tools will be referenced to support completion

4. ✍ **Journal With Me** — Invites deeper exploration through writing or quiet thought, helping you name what matters and what's next.

5. 💬 *Moving Thought* — Shares short truths to keep as mantras and intentions — quick reminders to ground and guide you.

M is for Motivation, Mindset & Make Space for Your Why

1. What This Letter Means

Every move begins with a reason.

It's already there — even if you can't name it yet.

Motivation is your why — the purpose that pulls you forward when the process seems hard.

Mindset is how you choose to see the journey — with openness, resilience, fear or self-trust.

Make space is the art of clearing room — physically and emotionally — so there is space for what's next.

Together these create the emotional and practical foundation of your Move Plan.
This is where intention begins, and uncertainty becomes direction.

2. 📖 Nia's Journey: Just Start

When Nia first sat down to outline her move, she wasn't sure what to write. Her mom had passed, the house felt too big, and she knew something had to change — but saying that out loud felt too abstract.

Instead of writing a full plan, she wrote a few truths and a few hopes. One of them was:

"I don't know if I'm moving away from something or toward something. Maybe both."

She didn't realize it then, but that sentence **was** her beginning.

3. Your Move Plan in Action

Motivation, mindset, and making space sets the tone for your entire move. This is where you capture the why behind your decisions —and make room, inside and out, for what comes next.

In your Move Plan, this section helps you define:

- What kind of move you're making

- Why now is the right time

- What you're truly hoping to shift, heal, or grow into

Move Plan Sections:

Move Name—What name gives your move identity and reflects your energy, intention, or hope?

Project Summary—How would you summarize your move in a few sentences right now?

Move Type—What type of move are you making—and does it fit one of the categories, or do you need to name your own?

Current Situation—What is your current situation—emotionally, physically, and logistically?

Goal of the Move—What specific change or result do you want this move to create?

Vision Statement + Success Statement—What do you want your space or life to feel like on the other side of this move?

If naming your move feels like a big first step, these tools are here to give you a place to begin.

✖ TOOL 2: Move Type and Vision Statement Worksheet

Helps you name what kind of move you're making and what your desired outcome looks like.

✗ TOOL 3: Name Your Move Worksheet

Helps you evaluate (or rename) your move title to reflect what feels true.

4. 🖎 Journal With Me

- What has called you to begin this move—internally or externally?

- What do you want to make space for in your life?

- If you had to title this chapter of your life, what would it be?

5. 💬 *Moving Thought*

You don't need the full picture to begin. You just need a name that feels honest today.

O is for Ownership, Organization & Creating Order Where There Is Chaos

1. What This Letter Means

This is the part of the move where chaos starts to meet clarity.

Before you sort a single room or delegate a single task, you have to define the structure—not just of your shelves, but of your story.

Ownership means recognizing this move belongs to you. It doesn't mean doing everything alone—it means leading with intention.

Organization is about arranging your thoughts, energy, and priorities so you can see clearly. It isn't just labeled bins and pretty calendars.

Order means deciding what matters most—what comes first, what can wait, and what no longer fits. It's not perfection.

Together, these three—ownership, organization, and order—build the framework of your Move Plan. They turn overwhelm into structure, and hesitation into progress.

2. 📖 Nia's Journey: From Surviving to Structuring

When I met Nia, she had been in survival mode for months. Her mother's house was full of memories, tasks, and decisions she didn't feel ready to face.

She kept saying she wasn't sure where to begin. What she didn't realize was that not deciding was also a decision—and it was costing her time, energy, and peace.

One afternoon, we sat down together and completed: the Move Readiness Check-In

Then we looked at her current reality: her timeline, her energy, the overall emotional weight of the move.

Instead of pushing through blindly, Nia claimed her next steps: she defined her Success Statement with a little prompting added how she would celebrate her progress.

This simple act gave her a plan—and with it the power she thought she had lost.

3. Your Move Plan in Action

Ownership, organization, and order give you more structure. They take the motivation you named in "M" and turn it into a plan you can actually follow.

In your Move Plan, this section helps you define:

- What decisions need structure—emotionally and logistically

- What roles and responsibilities you're carrying (and which ones you can release)

- What kind of order supports you—not just visually, but mentally and energetically

Move Plan Sections:

Current Situation: What is your current situation—emotionally, physically, and logistically?

Vision + Success Statement: What does meaningful progress and completion look like for this move?

Timeline + Key Milestones: What are the key milestones and deadlines that will guide your move?

Ownership begins with honesty. This tool helps you pause and check in with yourself before taking the next step.

✗ TOOL 4: Move Readiness Check-In

Helps you assess your energy, mindset, and emotional readiness.

4. ✍ Journal With Me

- Where in my move do I feel the most disorganized or overwhelmed?

- What assumptions have I been making about what I have to do alone?

- What would order look like for me — not just visually, but emotionally?

- What structure would help me lead with more clarity and less pressure?

- Who or what do I need to include to stay grounded and supported?

5. 💬 *Moving Thought*

Order isn't perfection.
It's permission — to organize your energy in a way that honors what matters most.

V is for Vision, Values & Voice — Let Values Lead Your Voice

1. What This Letter Means

Every move — whether physical, emotional, or aspirational — asks you to answer one question:

What are you building your next chapter around?

Values are core truths that shape your discussions and define what matters most.

Vision is the picture of the life and space you want to create.

Voice is the way you express those truths and advocate for what feels right.

When you are clear, your decisions become your blueprint:

- For what you keep

- For who you invite in

- For how your space — and life — feels moving forward

- For what you say yes — or no — to

Without clarity, it's easy to spiral into reactive choices: keeping too much, accepting help you don't need, or recreating a life that no longer fits.

This is your moment to stop and define your compass. Clarity here creates alignment later and reminds you that your voice matters.

2. 📖 Nia's Journey: From Empty Rooms to Intentional Living

Nia started with a vague wish:

"I want my space to feel lighter."

But "lighter" wasn't just about less clutter—it was about emotional weight.

When we explored it together, three values came to the surface:

- Adventure—She wanted to explore more, not just decorate more

- Self-love—She needed a bedroom that felt nurturing, not neutral

- Clarity—She wanted every room to have a purpose and a point

These values became her guide:

- She let go of the oversized sofa that dimmed the living room

- She repainted her mother's bedroom in soft pinks and creams

- She turned her desk to face the window, not the wall

Her values gave her permission to shape a space that felt like her next chapter—not her past.

3. Your Move Plan in Action

Vision, values, and voice shape the decisions that define your next chapter. This is where you make sure what you're creating aligns with what matters most—so every choice feels honest, intentional, and yours.

In your Move Plan this section helps you define:

- What you truly want from this move—physically, emotionally, and energetically

- What values you want your space and next chapter to reflect

- How to let your voice lead—so the decisions you make feel honest and aligned

These answers inform your:

Project Summary — If your move could speak in your true voice, what would it say about where you are headed?

Vision + Success Statement — What does a meaningful, values-aligned move look and feel like for you?

Self-Care + Stress Management — How will you care for yourself during this transition?

When it feels hard to put your vision into words. These tools help you speak it out loud and align it with what matters most.

🛠 TOOL 6: Value Mapping Tool

Helps you define how you want your life and space to feel after the move.

🛠 TOOL 7: 4-Box Sorting Tool

Guides you in naming the belongings and memories that matter most, tied to your values.

✗ TOOL 8: Legacy List Worksheet

Supports decisions about what to keep, release, donate, or hold for later—rooted in your values and vision.

4. ✍ Journal With Me

- What do I want to be true in my life after this move?

- What values matter most to me in this season?

- Where in my current space do I feel out of alignment?

- What needs to shift to help my space reflect who I am?

5. 💬 *Moving Thought*

A clear vision isn't about what your space looks like. It's about how your space helps you live.

I is for Insight, Involvement & Intuition —
Move with Mindfulness and Support

1. What This Letter Means

This part of your move invites you to **look inward and outward** — to name who is with you, to trust what you know, and to gather the insight that helps you move forward with confidence.

Involvement means identifying the people who will walk with **you — emotionally**, logistically, or spiritually.

Intuition is the quiet knowing within you. It helps you recognize what feels aligned and what doesn't — even when you can't explain why.

Insight is the wisdom that comes from reflection, experience, and asking the right questions at the right time.

Together, these three support **clarity, connection, and self-trust**.
They shape how you move — not just efficiently, but meaningfully.

This is the moment to:

- Name your key people

- Listen inward for your pace and rhythm

- Notice what your body and spirit are telling you

Involvement is about connection.
Intuition is about trust.
Insight is about remembering — you don't have to do this alone.

2. 📖 Nia's Journey: Slowing Down the Sort

Nia had a long to-do list — and her instinct was to power through it.

Clear the closets.
Empty the attic.
Check the boxes.

But the night before she began, something shifted.

She realized she wasn't just touching objects — she was touching *memories*.

So she paused.

She walked slowly through each room, naming what each space meant to her. She cried. She smiled. She wrote a few notes in her journal.

Only then did she begin — with intention:

- She created a playlist to keep her grounded

- She set time limits

- She took photos of items she wanted to remember but didn't need to keep

That was still sorting — but with presence.
That was implementation — but with heart.
That was intuition — in action.

3. Your Move Plan in Action

Involvement, intuition, and insight help you more with clarity and connection. This is where you name your people, trust your inner guardian, and identify what will keep you grounded along the way.

In your Move Plan this section helps you define:

• Who's part of your move—and how each person is supporting or influencing the process

• Where your intuition is guiding you—especially when decisions feel cloudy or emotional

• What you need to stay grounded, supported, and emotionally well during this transition

These answers inform your:

People Involved + Roles: Who's part of your move? What are they responsible for? How will you communicate with them?

Key Projects + Tasks: What actually needs to happen, and who is doing what? There's no single tool included for this section—use whatever task tracker, spreadsheet, or planner fits your style. What matters is clarity, not format.

Self-Care + Stress Management: What rituals and rhythms will support your emotional well-being? What matters most is honoring what actually supports you, not what you think should be doing.

Asking for help and trusting yourself don't always come easy. These tools are designed to help you balance both.

✘ TOOL 1: MOVING Method™ Tracker

Gives you a place to pause, notice, and capture what's happening—so you can check in with yourself as you go.

✘ TOOL 9: Moving Circle Worksheet

Helps you name the people and supports in your circle— so you don't have to move alone.

4. ✍ Journal With Me

- What emotional weight am I carrying into this move?

- What items feel sacred, sensitive, or tender — and why?

- What kind of support do I need, even if I haven't asked for it yet?

- What might shift if I allowed myself to move more slowly — or with more care?

- What am I actually trying to accomplish?

5. 💬 *Moving Thought*

Letting people in doesn't mean you're weak.
Letting your intuition lead doesn't mean you're lost.
This part of the move asks you to slow down, listen deeper, and trust that your next steps are allowed to feel tender.

You're not just sorting stuff — you're sorting stories.
Invite support. Honor what rises.
Move like it matters — because it does.

N is for Navigation & Next Steps — From Now to Next
Set the Course, Then Take the Next First Step

What This Letter Means

This part of the MOVING Method is about momentum — moving from reflection to action.

Navigation means setting your course. Not perfectly, but with presence. It's the shift from thinking to doing.

Now is your current reality — your energy, your circumstances, your capacity.

Next is the small step in front of you — the one that moves your plan forward.

You've made space. You've clarified your story. You've named your move and your circle.

Now it's time to make decisions — and take action.

Whether it's bold (listing the house) or small (booking a haul-away), what matters most is that your steps are grounded in your values, your vision, and your priorities for what comes next.

2. Nia's Journey: Planning Without Panic

Nia felt frozen when she looked at her list.
It wasn't the number of tasks — it was the fear that she would miss something important.

Her instinct was to try and control everything at once.
But control isn't the same as clarity.

Instead of starting with her whole house, we walked room by room.
We asked: *"What's the next right thing in this space?"*

We didn't try to do it all — we started with her kitchen.

- She created a zone for donation

- A box for legacy

- A drawer for daily use

It was simple.
It was doable.
And it gave her a win.

From there, we mapped her key projects, deadlines, and a realistic weekly schedule.

Once she knew what was next, the panic quieted.
She didn't need to finish everything in a day.
She just needed to know what mattered now.

3. Your Move Plan in Action

Navigation, now and next are about turning clarity into movement. This is where you map your course, anchor yourself in the present, and take the next right step toward your goal.

In your Move Plan this section helps you define:

- **What needs to happen next** — and in what order

- What's time-sensitive, what can wait, and what needs more clarity

- How to pace yourself realistically based on your current energy and capacity

Use the following sections of your Move Plan to bring this part of the method to life:

Timeline + Key Milestones: What are the key milestones and deadlines that will anchor your move?

Key Projects + Tasks: What major activities will move you forward, and how will you prioritize them?

Not every tool is a checklist. Sometimes the most powerful tool is the page in front of you. Journaling helps you slow down, notice what matters most, and choose the next right step with confidence.

4. ✍ Journal With Me

- What's something I've been putting off because I'm afraid to start?

- What would make my next step feel easier or more possible?

- What's one thing I've already done that I'm proud of?

- Where do I need structure—and where do I need flexibility?

- What are the top 3 things I need to complete first?

- Are there any dates, decision, or transitions I need to plan around?

- What spaces of categories feel urgent or time-sensitive?

- What would it mean to trust myself more fully in this move?

5. 💬 *Moving Thought*

You don't have to have it all figured out.
You just have to start.
One next right step at a time.

G is for Growth, Grounding & Grace – Becoming Through the Move

1. What This Letter Means

This final part of the MOVING Method invites you to reflect on how this transition has changed you.

Growth is the transformation that happens through the move — not always loud or dramatic, but often quiet, steady, and personal.

Grounding is what keeps you centered as life shifts. It's your anchor — your routines, rituals, and truths.

Grace is how you move through the process — with compassion, not perfection. It's what allows you to rest, release, and reset.

Together, these three remind you that every move is more than an ending — it's an opening.

This is where you:

- Look back and name what you've learned — honor progress

- Decide what you want to carry forward — stay rooted

- Let go of what no longer fits — seasons of change

You're not just moving out.
You're moving in — to your life.
And who you're becoming is just as important as where you're going.

2. 📖 Nia's Journey: Recognizing Her Becoming

After Nia moved her last box and lit a candle in her newly redesigned bedroom, she sat on the edge of her bed and realized something simple—but powerful:

She wasn't the same woman who began this move.

- She had learned how to make space for herself
- To say no
- To ask for help
- To live with grief and still choose joy

Growth didn't come from the plan.
It came from how she *lived through it*.

She wasn't just moving out of her mother's house.
She was moving into her own life.

3. Your Move Plan in Action

Growth, grounding and space are about capturing the changes this move has sparked in you—and choosing what you want to carry forward. This is where you pause to reflect on your inner shifts, honor the progress you've made, and set gentle practices to keep you rooted as you move ahead.

In your Move Plan, this section helps define:

- What personal growth this move has sparked or revealed

- What you're ready to release—physically, emotionally, or energetically

- How to stay grounded and offer yourself grace as you continue forward

This is the moment to reflect—and document—what has changed within you.

Move Plan Sections:

Goal of the Move: How has your original goal shifted through this process? What does it look like now?

Self-Care + Stress Management: What nourishes you at this point in the journey, and how will you care for your future self? If you've been tracking logistics, roles, and vision—this is where you honor your internal transformation.

Growth isn't about rushing—it's about returning. These tools invite you to pause, reflect, and move forward with grace.

⚒ TOOL 3: Name Your Move Worksheet

Helps you return to your move's name and see if it still reflects your direction.

⚒ TOOL 6: Value Mapping

Gives you space to revisit your vision and notice what has shifted or expanded.

⚒ TOOL 10: Letter to Your Future Self

Offers a moment of reflection to honor how far you've come and where you're going.

Growth takes practice—doing something over and over again until it becomes part of you.

But moving is different. Most of us don't do it often enough to master it.

Instead, each move leaves us with a lesson:

about what we carried, what we let go of, and who we became along the way.

Journaling is where those lessons live,

so they don't get lost in the boxes or the chaos.

It's how you notice your own becoming.

4. ✍ Journal With Me

- What has this move taught me about resilience, clarity, or boundaries?

- Where did I surprise myself?

- What patterns or beliefs did I release?

- How will I honor the version of me that showed up through this process?

- What rituals or small acts of care will help me stay grounded?

5. 💬 *Moving Thought*

Growth doesn't always announce itself.
Sometimes, it whispers:
"Look at who you are now."

Putting It All Together: Your Move, Your Method

You've just done something powerful.

You've walked through the full MOVING Method™—
six letters, six touchpoints, six invitations to move with
more clarity, intention, and grace.

Maybe you've started filling out your Move Plan.
Maybe you've just begun to imagine what's possible.

Either way, you've taken a meaningful step.

And that's the truth about the MOVING Method:
It's not about doing everything at once.
It's about returning to each part—when you need it, how
you need it, as you grow.

Let this be a living tool.

- Come back to "M" when you feel stuck.

- Reread "V" when you lose sight of your values.

- Lean on "G" to remind yourself that even small steps
  are signs of growth.

Your Move Plan will keep evolving—just like you.

💬 *Moving Thought*

Moving well isn't about getting everything right.
It's about showing up—again and again—with courage,
clarity, and care.

CHAPTER 6:
Gather What You Need
A Straightforward Guide to What Works—
Before It Gets Overwhelming

Let's be clear: this chapter isn't about feelings. You've already done the inner work—named your move, started your plan, and clarified your goals. Now it's time to pause, reflect, and lean into action.

This isn't about your "why," your fear, or your vision.

This is where you stop spinning and start stacking—boxes, plans, and actual decisions.

Inside you'll find real answers to the most common (and confusing) questions people face during a move or estate clearing. It's a lot of what I wish people knew before things got hard.

Along the way I've gathered a few of my hard-earned truths—short phrases I've said to clients (and myself) in the middle of a move. They are kind-of reminders that cut through the noise and get you back on track.

Take what you need. Leave the rest. But don't skip this part.

Because you can't move forward with clarity if you haven't gathered what grounds you.

20 Reminders to Move with Clarity

These aren't rules—they're reminders. Some I've learned the hard way. Others I've said out loud so many times, they've become part of my method. You'll know them when you feel them.

1. **Don't Shop Your Way Through a Breakdown.** Buying can feel like control when everything else feels uncertain. Retail therapy adds clutter, not clarity. Take a breath. Pause before the purchase.

2. **Don't Shop While You're Moving.** Do not bring new stuff into a space you're trying to leave. Shop your own house first. Make a post-move wishlist. Lead with the plan — not the panic.

3. **Use Your Trash Day Like It's Your Accountability Partner.** The garbage truck shows up every week — so should your momentum. Let it be a nudge not a guilt trip. Treat it like a moving deadline.

4. **The Decision Is Already Made. Trust It.** If you've touched it five times, your gut already knows. No need to overprocess. Let the first instinct guide the choice.

5. **Not Every Item Deserves Your Energy.** Save your strength for what tells your story. If it doesn't spark a sentence, it may not be worth saving.

6. **You're Not Purging — You're Preparing.** Letting go isn't about loss — it's about alignment. You're not just clearing space. You're making room for who you're becoming.

7. **Start With the Whole Picture.** Before you touch a single item, take in the entire space. Walk each room. Make notes. Build a plan around *capacity*, not chaos.

8. **Build a Let-Go Rhythm With Trash & Recycling.** Use your city's schedule to keep things moving. One bag a week. One box at a time. Let routine do the work.

9. **Who You Donate To Matters.** Donating is emotional, not just logistical. Give where it aligns. That's how you release with peace.

10. **Timeline Truths (That Might Surprise You).** Moves take longer when emotions are involved—and they always are. Reverse engineer your plan. Add time for feelings, not just packing.

11. **Set Decision Boundaries.** At some point, you need to stop deciding and start doing. Pick a "no more rethinking" date. Then stick to it like moving day.

12. **Estate Clearing? Use These Four Phases.** Legacy work is sacred—and hard. Secure → Survey → Decide → Distribute. Grace over guilt.

13. **Keep the Paper That Keeps You Moving.** Not all paper is clutter—but not all of it matters. Create a Transition Folder for essentials only. Shred the rest with confidence.

14. **Most Supplies Are Just More Clutter.** Buying storage containers won't fix the mess—it just hides it. Start with what you already have. Get clear before you get cute.

15. **Simple Tech That Keeps You Sane.** Let your phone hold the chaos so you don't have to. Use reminders, notes, and tracking apps to save your peace.

16. Don't Go It Alone. You are not meant to carry this by yourself. Build your Moving Circle. Ask for real help.

17. Without a Plan, It's Just Piles and Panic. Structure doesn't kill freedom—it creates it. Start small. But *start* with a plan.

18. Your Old Friends Can't Help You Move. The pizza-for-labor era is over. This is grown-folk heavy. Ask with clarity or hire help.

19. Clutter Is Like Gremlins. There's always more hiding in the shadows. Just when you think you're done, you'll open one more drawer. That doesn't mean you failed—it means you're *really* looking. Stay curious, not discouraged. You're making progress.

20. It's Not a Collection If It's Not Displayed. If it's hidden in a box, it's not honoring the story—it's hoarding it. Curate what you love. Let it be seen, shared, and celebrated.

These reminders aren't just about stuff—they're about *how* you show up to the work of moving. Whether you're packing boxes, making decisions, or just trying not to shut the door and walk away, keep them close.

Because the real work isn't just clearing space—it's claiming it.

💬 *Moving Thought*

What I bring to Day One:

When I show up at a client's home, I don't just bring bins and labels.

I bring calm.
I bring clarity.
I bring a quiet confidence that we will figure it out — together.

Here's what I always carry in:

- *A clipboard with a Move Plan (even if it's rough)*

- *Notes about what matters to you*

- *Labels, Post-its, and painter's tape*

- *A flexible plan and a deep respect for your pace*

Here's what I hope we build:

- *A clear picture of the full space — not just the "problem area"*

- *A shared sense of timeline and capacity*

- *A safe partnership to ask hard questions and make bold decisions*

Because moving isn't just about getting through it.
It's about getting free on the other side of it.

So whether I'm standing next to you — or you're walking through this with the book — I hope this chapter gave you:

Not just answers, but authority.
Not just plans, but permission.

Let's get it done — with grace, not grind.

CHAPTER 7:
Moving with Fear—
Making Room for Truth, Tenderness, and Trust

You've gathered the tools. Made the lists. Created a plan that feels intentional, maybe even doable.

But even with structure in place, something else always shows up. Not loudly. Not all at once. Just beneath the surface—waiting.

That something is fear.

Not the kind that slams the brakes. But the kind that makes you second-guess your strength. That questions your choices. That whispers: Are you sure? Are you ready?

Let's talk about it. Not to get rid of it—but to make room for truth, tenderness, and trust.

Nia's Journey: The Room She Feared

For Nia, it happened as she stood frozen at the threshold of her mother's bedroom. Her hand rested on the doorknob, her breath caught in her throat. She had packed the garage, sorted the kitchen, even scheduled the donation truck—but this room whispered her name at night and dared her to open the drawers.

This wasn't just a room. It was grief wrapped in cotton sweaters and perfume bottles.

And this was the moment fear showed up.

Nia heard the voice rise within her:
"What if I break down?"
"What if I throw something important away?"
"What if my siblings judge me?"
"What if I lose pieces of her?"

She didn't argue. She responded:
"Then I'll pause. Breathe. Ask for help." "I've already decided what matters. My values are my filter—not guilt." "I'm not doing this for approval. I'm doing it to reclaim peace." "I already carry the best parts of her in me. I don't need to carry it all."

And with that, Nia walked in. Not fearless. But faithful. She didn't push fear out of the room. She made space for it—beside her, not ahead of her.

Fear didn't disappear for Nia that day—it shifted. She saw it for what it was and answered it with truth.

Fear shows up differently in every move. This chart shows how it threads through the MOVING Method™ and where it connects back to your Move Plan.

The Roles of Fear in the MOVING Method™

MOVING Letter	How Fear Shows Up	What It Needs	Move Plan Connection
M	"What if I'm making the wrong move?"	Reconnect with your story	Project Summary
O	" Where do I even begin with all this?"	Name what is real.	Current Situation
V	"If I follow my needs, I'll disappoint others."	Anchor in values instead of approval	Vision + Success Statement
I	"No one will understand me."	Define your Moving Circle with intention	People Involved + Roles
N	"I'll never get it all done."	Focus on the next right step	Timeline + Key Projects
G	"What if I do all this and nothing changes?"	Ground yourself in the goal and give yourself permission to move forward	Goal of the Move

📖 Nia's Journey: Fear as a Member of the Moving Circle

For Nia, that truth became personal. Fear wasn't gone – it simply found its place. She gave it She gave it a seat at the table – but not the clipboard.

Because here's the truth: Fear is part of your team. It belongs in the room. But it doesn't get to lead the process.

When you treat fear like a quiet voice – not a screaming monster – you reclaim your power. You get to say:

"Thank you for the warning. But I'm moving anyway."

That's presence.

Presence isn't pretending you're not afraid – it's recognizing fear, nodding to it, and choosing to keep going anyway.

Fear can walk with you. But presence leads the way.

Presence sounds like your breath slowing. Your hands unclenching. Your ability to stay connected to the moment instead of reacting to the fear.

Fear is part of your Moving Circle. It gets a seat, not the steering wheel. Presence is the voice that checks in before charging ahead. It reminds every part of you – including fear – that all voices matter. But not every voice leads.

🛠 TOOL 9 – Moving Circle Worksheet

Map your circle so even fear has a place — without steering the move.

✍️ Journal with Me

- What fear am I carrying quietly but consistently?

- Where does fear tend to show up in my move—decisions, letting go, timing, asking for help?

- What have I done even though I was afraid?

- What would support look like if I honored my fear instead of hiding it?

You can name fear. You can even welcome it. But on moving day—when the doorbell rings, the memories hit, or the attic door creaks open—you'll need something more than presence. You'll need a way to respond.

That's what this next section offers: not solutions, but practices. Six small ways to meet fear without giving it the lead role.

Six Ways to Respond When Fear Shows Up
These aren't fixes. They're practices. Repeat as needed.

1. **Name It Early**
   When fear is unnamed, it becomes background noise.
   Example: *"I'm afraid this item will bring up memories I'm not ready to feel."*
   Pro Tip: Write one fear at the top of your Move Plan. Naming it can bring relief.

2. **Give It a Job—But Not the Lead Role**
   Fear often tries to protect you. Let it, but on your terms.

Example: *"Fear, you're here to help me slow down. But I'm leading the plan."*
Pro Tip: If something feels too emotional to do alone, assign a helper for that task.

3. Practice the Pause

When fear shows up as panic or spiraling, pause before you act (or avoid). Ask yourself: *"What's the kindest next step I can take right now?"*
Pro Tip: Pair this with a grounding action — deep breath, stretch, or stepping outside for air — before you decide.

4. Track Your Wins

Fear forgets progress — you need to remind it. Keep a list in your Move Journal of "moments I showed up anyway."
Example:
• *Sorted Mom's books, even though I cried.*
• *Said no to someone else's timeline.*
• *Paused instead of pushing through.*
Pro Tip: Review your list before tackling a tough task to remind yourself you've done hard things before.

5. Create a Fear Checkpoint

Build fear-awareness into your Move Plan. Add a weekly "Fear Check-In" section:
• What fear showed up this week?
• How did it affect my actions or thoughts?
• How did I respond?
• What support or shift do I need next week?
Pro Tip: Schedule this checkpoint in your calendar so it becomes a steady ritual, not just a good idea.

6. Return to the Plan

Fear makes everything feel like chaos. Go back to your MOVE Plan. Take one small step you've already decided on and let your past clarity guide you forward.
Pro Tip: Mark your next task in bold or with a star so you can find it fast when fear clouds your focus.

Unpack: A Moment with Fear.

Fear is a shape-shifter. Sometimes it sounds like a whisper; other times, like a door slamming shut. Before you move forward, pause here.

What is one fear that's quietly shaping how you're approaching this move? Write it down without judgment. Then, write a grounded response. Not to silence it—but to honor what's real and remind yourself who's in charge.

You don't have to evict fear. You just don't have to hand it the keys.

 Moving Thought

"Fear isn't the problem. Silence is. Give fear a voice— but not a microphone. Let it be part of the conversation, not the director of the move."

Spoken fears lose power. Shared fears build connection.

You don't need to be fearless to move. You just need to move with intention—and give fear its proper seat.

CHAPTER 8:
The Weight of Stuff—
Understanding the Cost of What We Carry

After fear speaks, the stuff starts to speak louder.

You've named the emotions. You've slowed down enough to listen. But then comes the moment you touch your things—open the drawers, lift the boxes, find the scarf or the letter that takes your breath away.

That's when the weight shows up.

Not just physical weight—though there's plenty of that. This is the weight of what we carry emotionally, and more importantly, the stories we tell ourselves about *why* we carry it. Because it's never just about the stuff. It's about memory. Identity. Expectation.

This chapter is where we name that weight, understand its cost, and begin to release it with clarity, compassion, and care.

There are more than 300,000 items in the average American home. It sounds impossible—until you start packing. Until you open every drawer. Touch every object. Face every I'll-deal-with-it-later.

Moving forces a reckoning. It's one of the only times in life when you come face-to-face with everything you've carried—in your hands, in your heart, and in the shadows of your past selves.

That weight isn't random. It follows patterns I see again and again—each with its own emotional story. And when we can name what kind of clutter we're facing, we begin to understand how to release it.

The Three Types of Clutter

Physical Clutter—The visible stuff. Overflowing closets, stacked bins, and duplicate kitchen tools. It takes up space, time, and energy. Example: The Tupperware collection that's followed you through four moves.

Emotional Clutter—The invisible weight. Items tied to grief, guilt, identity, or a former version of yourself. Often the hardest to release. Example: Your grandmother's dishes that live in boxes, not cabinets.

Aspirational Clutter—The "someday" items. Representing who you thought you'd be, what you hoped to do, or how you wanted to live. They don't always match your present self. Example: The guitar you bought five years ago that's still in the case.

You now have a way to define the clutter. Now let's talk about the weight. Not the kind you measure on a scale—but the kind you feel in your chest, your calendar, your memories.

Look around. The weight is already here. Let's name it.

Because this isn't just about what you see. **What surrounds you often reflects what's happening inside you.** Your stuff speaks for you. It holds grief you haven't processed. Dreams you haven't lived. Guilt you didn't know you carried.

When you don't have space—or language—to express something, it can show up as clutter. And when you've lived with too much for too long, it becomes hard to know what's worth keeping.

Let's name the weight. Because before you can let it go, you have to understand what it is. The more you carry, the more it costs—not just in space, but in spirit. And sometimes, the heaviest things don't even fit in a box.

These weights aren't failures. They're evidence that you've lived, loved, and now you're in the middle of letting go.

Giving language to what you're carrying makes it easier to release. Naming the type of weight helps you choose your next move. Each one calls for a different kind of support—and a different kind of release.

The Six Types of Weight

Emotional Weight—What you feel in your chest. Grief, regret, identity shifts. It often ties directly to memories or losses that haven't been processed.

Mental Weight—What you feel in your head. Decision fatigue, overwhelm, perfectionism. The cognitive load of constant choice-making and uncertainty.

Energetic Weight—What you feel in your body. Avoidance, cluttered environments that drain your spirit. A lack of peace or clarity.

Relational Weight—What you feel in your relationships. Tensions over shared items, expectations from family, or guilt tied to other people's memories.

Financial Weight—What you feel in your wallet and mind. The cost of keeping, storing, replacing, or moving items—and the pressure to "make it all work."

Physical Weight— What you feel in your body size, strength, and stamina. Sometimes it's the literal heaviness of what you're carrying. Sometimes its the stress weight, the holding it all in weight, the way your body shifts when everything is in motion.

These six weights often show up together—and they each speak a different language. But naming them gives you power. More clarity. More room to move.

So what does this look like in real time? Here's how weight shows up during a move—and what it leads to:

- **Grief and Loss**—You avoid making decisions and leave certain rooms untouched *so that* you don't have to reopen the pain of what's been lost. But this often prolongs the process and makes letting go harder later.

- **Fear of the Unknown**—You delay decisions because stepping into a future you can't yet see feels risky. *So that* becomes staying in place longer than necessary—clinging to the familiar, even when it no longer fits.

- **Decision Fatigue**—You get overwhelmed by constant choices—what stays, what goes, what matters. *So that* everything stays, making your move more expensive, delayed, or scattered.

- **Identity Shifts**—You aren't sure who you are now or who you want to become in this next chapter. *So that* you hold onto old roles, clothes, or routines—even when they no longer serve you.

- **Loneliness**—You feel emotionally alone, even when people are around. *So that* you isolate further during a time when support could lighten the load.

- **Physical Exhaustion**—You're tired in your bones. But instead of asking for help, you push through. *So that* the move becomes harder than it needs to be, and burnout sets in.

- **Financial Pressure**—You stretch your resources to make everything work. *So that* even simple decisions feel high-stakes, and the weight of each dollar adds emotional strain.

- **Perfectionism**—You try to make the move look effortless. *So that* others don't see the unraveling underneath—but the cost is your own peace and permission to be real.

These aren't just passing feelings. They're real weights—felt in your back, your breath, your boxes, and your budget.

Every item carries something:
- A story
- A cost
- A decision you're either making—or avoiding

✍️ Journal with Me: What Are You Carrying?

Take a moment to slow down here. Reflect on the following:

- What items do you feel most conflicted about? Why is it hard to let go?

- Which category do those items fall into? Physical, emotional, or aspirational clutter?

- What story does this item tell? Does it still serve your present or future self?

- What would it feel like to release it? Name the emotion.

Unpack: Pause and Plan for Dispersal

Every item that doesn't align with your vision has a future beyond you. Letting go doesn't mean discarding. It means rehoming, recycling, donating, or honoring with intention.

Ask:

- Can this item bless someone else?
- Is there a local charity, shelter, or artist who could use it?
- Would a photo and a short, written memory help you release it?

 Jevata-ism Let your release be a ritual, not just a task.

⚒ TOOL # 7: 4-Part Sorting Method

Use this tool to make clear, intentional choices and what stays, what goes, and what moves forward.

💬 *Moving Thought*

Stuff carries memory, identity, and emotion—but you get to decide what travels forward. Let go of what weighs you down. Keep what lifts you up. That's how you lighten your move—and your life.

CHAPTER 9:
Lonely Boxes and Finding Your Circle

Lonely Boxes

Boxes don't talk back.
They don't ask how you're doing.
They just wait.
Quiet.
Heavy.
Unopened.

You can be surrounded by stuff
and still feel completely alone.
No one sees the tears you cry
in the hallway between sorting
     and keeping.
No one feels the ache in
     your chest
when you tape shut a memory.

Moving isn't just about lifting.
It's about letting go.
And that shouldn't happen
     alone.

You deserve more than silence.
You deserve support.

A voice that says,
"I've got you."
A presence that says,
"You don't have to do this
     all by yourself."

Because moving is hard.
But it's less lonely
when someone else carries
     even a corner of the box.

If you've ever felt that kind of silence—the kind where boxes surround you but no one really sees you—this chapter is for you. Because moving isn't just a task. It's a tender, complicated transition. And no one should have to do it alone.

Unpack: The Silence Between the Tasks

Moving is often seen as a solo sport. But silence can be heavy, too.

This is your pause before the next push.
Before the next box.
Before the next brave decision.

Ask yourself:

- Do I want to do this alone—or am I just used to it?
- What kind of help would feel grounding—not just useful?
- What do I need—not later, but right now?

You don't have to know all the answers. You just have to stop long enough to ask.

This chapter begins not with doing, but with choosing: to invite support, to name your needs, and to honor that asking for help is part of moving well.

From Isolation to Intention

The move isn't lighter because it's easy. It's lighter because you chose not to carry it alone.

You can be surrounded by boxes and still feel alone. Moving has a way of isolating you—not because people don't care, but because they often don't see the depth of what you're carrying. The silence between decisions, the fear that shows up at 2 a.m., the ache of doing it all yourself. That's what we're naming in this chapter — and that's where your circle comes in.

⭐ **Jevata-ism**

"Not everyone gets access. Your Moving Circle is earned, not inherited."

Choose people who honor your pace, your process, and your peace.

Defining Your Moving Circle

Your Moving Circle is your support team: the people, professionals, and resources you intentionally gather to help you navigate this transition — physically, emotionally, and logistically. It's not about who's available. It's about who aligns with your energy, your needs, and your values.

This isn't just about hiring movers or calling your most organized friend. Support doesn't always come in the form of friends and family — and it doesn't have to. Sometimes the most grounding presence in your Moving Circle is someone you've hired. Professional support is still personal support when it helps carry the weight.

This is about choosing people who can hold space for your process, not just your boxes.

You might need:

Before the Move: Emotional Grounding & Planning Support
- A close friend who asks the hard questions.
- A therapist, coach, or spiritual guide.
- A move manager or organizer to help you plan.

During the Move: Logistical & Hands-On Help
- Movers, packers, and drivers.
- Friends or family who help sort, carry, or clean.
- Someone to manage meals, errands, or childcare.

After the Move: Integration & Emotional Recovery
- Someone who checks in once the adrenaline fades.
- A professional who helps you set up your space.
- A friend who helps you celebrate how far you've come.

You don't need a crowd. You just need the right people in the right roles—people who help you carry not just what's in your hands, but what's on your heart.

Nia's Journey: The Loneliest Room in the House

Nia didn't ask for help until her body gave out. She told herself she could handle it—just one more box, one more load, one more night of sorting alone.

She kept saying, *"I've got it."*
But the truth was, she didn't.
Not all of it. Not anymore.

There was one room she couldn't face—her mother's bedroom. Every time she walked past the door, her chest tightened. She stacked boxes outside it, convincing herself she'd "get to it tomorrow."

But tomorrow never came.

It wasn't until her neighbor knocked and found her sitting on the floor—surrounded by half-packed memories and unopened grief—that she finally said the words that changed everything: *"I don't think I can do this by myself."*

Her neighbor didn't offer a solution. She just sat down beside her. Sometimes that's all the help you need: presence, not fixing. After that moment, Nia began building her circle—not out of ease, but out of necessity.

Her move didn't get easier overnight. But it stopped feeling so lonely.

✐ Journal with Me: Who's Helping You?

Before you invite others into your circle, take a moment to turn inward. These questions are here to help you clarify what support you need—and how to ask for it.

• What do I most want to feel supported in right now?

• Where have I been pretending I don't need help?

• Who do I already trust to show up with care?

• What kind of presence would feel grounding in this season of transition?

Be Thoughtful with Your Team: Interviewing Your Circle

Choosing your circle is an intentional part of moving well. Be thoughtful about who gets access to your process.

Core Questions:

- What do you understand about the kind of move I'm making?
- How do you handle emotional conversations or change?
- What kind of support do you feel most comfortable offering?

For Friends or Family:

- How do you see your role in this process?
- What do you need from me to feel supported in that role?

For Professionals:

- How do you work with clients in transition?
- What's your communication style during high-stress periods?

Tools That Keep Support Flowing

Support doesn't just show up—it needs structure. Your Moving Circle works best when you give them tools to stay connected, coordinated, and clear. These aren't just logistics—they're love in action.

- Shared Spreadsheets—Track tasks, dates, and roles using tools like Google Sheets or Airtable.

- Group Chats—Create a dedicated thread for updates, questions, and encouragement.

- Shared Calendars—Coordinate availability for packing sessions, pickups, or emotional check-ins.

• Labels & Zones—Use signs, colors, or folders to visually reduce decision fatigue.

• Copy of the Move Plan—Share a simplified version with your core people so they know what's coming.

✖ TOOL 5: Move Plan Template
Share a simplified version with your Moving Circle to keep everyone informed and aligned.

✖ TOOL 9: Moving Circle Worksheet
Helps you define who's on your support team, what role they play, and how to communicate your needs.

✪ Jevata-ism

Small systems = big clarity. This is how you stay rooted instead of reactive

---

💬 *Moving Thought*

You don't have to wait until you break to ask for help. Support isn't just for the moment when the box gets too heavy. It's for the moment before— the one where your heart whispers, "I can't keep doing this alone."

Let someone sit beside you. Let your circle begin there.

CHAPTER 10:
Unpacking What You Are Carrying

There's a quiet moment after the final box is brought in.

The truck has pulled away, the helpers have said goodbye, and you're left standing in your new space—surrounded by pieces of your old life packed inside cardboard walls.

This is your in-between.

This is also your reset.

A chance to stop surviving the move and start living in your place.

This is where you shift from wrapping up the past to shaping what comes next.
You're not just unpacking boxes—you're reintroducing yourself to your life.

The physical move may be technically complete, but the transformation is not. This is when the real work of becoming begins. What happens next will either reinforce old patterns or open the door to something beautifully aligned with the life you're building.

In the last chapter, we talked about your Moving Circle—the team that helped you navigate the logistics, the emotion, and the resistance. That role is not complete now that the move is "done." This next phase may ask for even more vulnerability, because now it's just you and your choices. Your environment is about to become an honest reflection of who you are and what you value.

Even though the boxes are in and the keys are yours, this isn't a solo chapter. Your Circle might shift—maybe they become your sounding board for decorating, your reminder to rest, or simply the friend who helps you laugh when you feel overwhelmed. Keep letting yourself be supported. Becoming is not a task to check off—it's a process to be held onto.

⭐ **Jevata-ism**

How you unpack is just as important as how you packed.

Choose Intentional Unpacking

Unpacking is a choice. It doesn't always happen right away—or at all.
Some people live surrounded by boxes for weeks, months, even years. Not from laziness, but from overwhelm, exhaustion, or uncertainty about where to begin.

Choosing to unpack, even slowly and imperfectly, is choosing to step into your next chapter. It's a way of saying: I belong here. I'm ready to make this space home.

If you packed with care—naming your values and letting go of what no longer serves you—unpacking becomes an act of clarity. But even if your boxes were filled in a rush, through tears, or "just to get through the day," you still have a second chance. You can choose now to unpack with intention.

 TOOL 6: Value Mapping Tool

Use this tool to align what you unpack, reset or reclaim with the values you named earlier.

Nia's Journey: A Room of Her Own

Nia stood in the doorway of her new home—keys in hand, sun pouring through the windows, silence echoing back a welcome. The house was still mostly empty except for a few boxes stacked neatly against the wall. Her body ached in places she didn't know could ache, but her spirit was light.

She had done it.

Clearing her mother's home had meant sorting through layers of grief and memory—some sweet, others sharp, all sacred. Every photograph, every dish, every letter folded in a drawer had asked her: Are you ready to let go? After months of decisions and tears, she had released what she needed to and carried forward what mattered most.

From her "Open First" box, she pulled the letter she had written to herself at the start of this journey:

> Dear Me,
>
> You are allowed to start over. This is not abandonment—it's becoming. Choose what nourishes you now. You do not have to carry everything to be whole.
>
> Love, Nia

The words landed differently now. Back then, they had felt like hope. Today, they felt like truth.

She lit the candle tucked beside the letter, opened a window, and let the breeze roll in—fresh and full of possibility. Anita Baker's voice floated from her playlist, followed by Sade and Grover Washington, Jr. Her shoulders softened.

Not everything needed to come inside. She had set aside boxes with colorful tape—the "hold" pile—items she thought were nonnegotiable but now realized needed another look.

Before letting anything in, she paused to ask: Does this reflect who I'm becoming? Or just who I've been?

She didn't rush. She didn't force it. She let her pace become a conversation—with her past, her present, and the future she was beginning to trust.

She picked up a photo of her mother—the one that always made her laugh—and set it gently on the mantle.

"I'm here," she whispered.

The house, as if listening, whispered back: Welcome.

She didn't unpack everything that first evening, but she did make one corner hers. She laid down her favorite rug, lit a candle, and placed her journal and a framed photo beside a soft chair.

It wasn't just neat—it felt intentional. That one simple space whispered: You belong here now. Her nervous system began to settle. She wasn't just in a house. She was beginning to come home—finding a corner of her own

🔨 TOOL 10: Letter to Your Future Self

Write a letter you can return to later, reminding yourself of what matters most when the move feels heavy.

Six Ways to Unpack With Intention

Clearing space creates peace.
Lesson: Clearing boxes and opening surfaces signals safety, allowing your body to shift from "threat mode" to rest.

Example: Nia noticed her shoulders drop once her kitchen counters were clear of cardboard.
Pro Tip: Start with one surface—a nightstand, a table, or a shelf—and let that small win reset your system.

Unpacking releases what you no longer need.
Lesson: Each item you unpack is a story you've chosen to carry forward—or release.
Example: As Nia unwrapped her mother's teacup, she placed it on her own shelf with gratitude, no longer weighed down by the rest of the set.
Pro Tip: Keep a "gratitude box" nearby for items you're ready to release, and let it remind you that letting go is an act of love too.

Every intentional choice makes space for delight.
Lesson: Unpacking with intention makes room for fresh experiences and rituals.
Example: Nia set up her morning coffee corner—mug, journal, and candle—turning it into her first new ritual at home.
Pro Tip: Pick one daily practice you want to nurture, and unpack that space first.

Each box cleared is a step forward.
Lesson: Every time you finish a box or a corner, you reinforce that the move is manageable.
Example: Nia felt lighter after finishing just one box in her bedroom—proof she didn't have to do it all at once.
Pro Tip: Break the work into time blocks or categories instead of whole rooms to see steady progress.

What you unpack first reveals what matters most.
Lesson: Choosing what to unpack first reflects who you are becoming, not just what you own.
Example: Nia prioritized her bookshelf, filling it with titles that spoke to adventure and self-love.
Pro Tip: Unpack items that connect to your values before décor or extras—you'll feel more at home right away.

Small spaces of intention create belonging.
Lesson: Creating intentional pockets of comfort helps
transform a house into a sanctuary.
Example: Nia laid her favorite rug, lit a candle, and placed a
framed photo in her reading corner—it instantly felt like hers.
Pro Tip: Designate one "anchor corner" early, so you have
a place to retreat and recharge while the rest of the house
comes together

 Unpack: Tune Into Your Space

Stand in the heart of your home. Take a slow breath in,
letting your eyes scan the room. Then close them. Where do
you feel tension—physical or emotional? If that area were
clear and organized, how might you feel differently?

Intentional unpacking means placing items not by habit,
but by purpose—where your values and vision meet your
everyday routines.

It's not enough to choose values that feel inspiring—you
need to know exactly what they mean to you.
Because when the move gets messy... when fear creeps in...
when you feel stuck...
Your values are your anchors.

If you've defined them in your own words, you'll know how
to return to them.

 Nia's Journey: Values in Action

Nia stood in her new living room, eyeing the pile of boxes
labeled "Misc." She laughed to herself—*Miscellaneous* had
always been code for "I didn't want to decide."

This time, she grabbed her journal and wrote Clarity at the
top of the page.
One by one, she opened each box and decided where every

item belonged. No holding pen. No "maybe later." She pictured the space she wanted and kept only what fit that vision.

Halfway through, she found her old hiking backpack. It reminded her of the trip she'd been promising herself for years. She smiled—Adventure was going back on the calendar. She set the pack in a place she'd see it every day.

By the end, her boxes were empty, her shelves intentional. This was more than organizing. It was Self-Love in action—keeping the things that let her life feel like hers.

Clarity: A desk or corner for planning, bills, and journaling.
Self-Love: A cozy nook with soft textiles for rest and reflection.
Adventure: A shelf or wall display for maps, travel mementos, or creative tools.

✍ Journal with Me: Organize with Purpose

- Write down the values you've chosen for this move.

- Next to each, write a short definition—in your own words.

- Why did you choose this value?

- How will it guide your decisions when things get hard?

MOVING Method™ Alignment: Living into Your Space

Letter	Focus Area	Unpacking Lens
M	Transition from "getting it done" to "living with purpose."	What feeling do I want this space to hold?
O	Take responsibility for how your space supports you.	Am I choosing this layout because it works for me, or because I feel I should?
V	Let zones, décor, and flow reflect the life you want to live.	Does what I see here match what I want to see every day?
I	Be fully present in the decisions you're making.	Does this arrangement feel right for how I live?
N	Create systems and flow that make daily life easier.	How will I move through this room? What supports that movement?
G	Allow your space to evolve with you.	Does this setup leave room for change?

Don't just think about these questions—walk through your space with them.

• **Touch:** Open a drawer, move a chair, fold a blanket.

• **See:** Step back and notice what draws your eye—is it what you want to see every day?

• **Feel:** Check in with your body—do you tense up, or exhale?

• **Hear:** What does this space sound like when you're in it? Music? Quiet? Chaos?

Your answers aren't abstract. They're living in the room with you. The more you notice, the more your space will feel like a place you've moved into—not just moved through.

💬 *Moving Thought*

Unpacking is sacred. When I work with clients during this phase, I'm not just helping them unpack and organize— I'm helping them land. I witness the shift from uncertainty to clarity, from "just moved in" to "I belong here."

Each box we open holds more than things—it holds decisions, energy, and possibility. Together, we create spaces that support who they're becoming. That's not just my job. That's my honor.

CHAPTER 11:

When a Season of Change Becomes a Method

By now, you've unpacked more than just boxes—you've started making space for a new version of yourself. You've cleared, chosen, and created with intention. And now, we step back.

In this chapter, I want to show you where the MOVING Method came from—not just emotionally, but practically. You've experienced how it works. Here, I'll show you how it was built. Because what you've been walking through isn't just a personal shift—it's the same framework I used to build a business, serve clients, and transform my life.

You've already seen how the MOVING Method came from lived experience. This chapter zooms out—not to tell the story again, but to show how instinct, repetition, and service turned into something structured, scalable, and deeply purposeful. This is not just the backstory of Project MOVE—it's the blueprint of how real transitions shape real frameworks.

Turning the Chaos into Clarity

I didn't set out to start a business. I didn't even set out to organize anyone's life, not even my own. I said yes when people asked me for help—first one friend, then another. Each time, I brought what I had: structure, patience, questions, and snacks.

I used the same tools I'd relied on in my corporate work: spreadsheets, coordination, and timeline management. I thought I was just helping. But something deeper was happening.

As I helped others move through transition, I realized I was creating a rhythm—one that turned overwhelm into action. I noticed:

- People needed structure when everything feels chaotic.

- People needed encouragement when self-doubt crept in.

- People needed questions that invited not just action — but reflection.

That's when I started tracking what worked — not because I had a vision for a brand, but because I saw something repeatable. I was building a methodology without knowing it.

I didn't name it right away. But I was already living it.

When the Move Became a Method

As word spread, people started asking for help. But they didn't say, "Can you help me move?" They said, "I don't need a mover — I need you."

That was the moment I understood this was more than logistics. I wasn't just lifting boxes — I was lifting the weight of transition.

That clarity marked the shift: I wasn't just helping. I was offering a service.

That's when I began to document and define what I had been doing:
- What steps worked, in what order.
- What questions created breakthroughs.
- What emotional moments disrupted the flow, and how to hold space for them.

This wasn't about inventing something. It was about naming what I had already practiced — and refining it into something teachable and repeatable.

From Practice to Process: Naming the MOVING Method

Giving the method a name gave it shape and power. Remember how I say it is important to give your move a name. Naming my process, MOVING Method, gave it power. Not from a single moment of brilliance, but move by move, client by client, one small insight at a time.

The MOVING Method isn't static. It adapts. It flexes. It meets people where they are. That's what makes it work.

Each letter in the MOVING Method holds layers—rooted in experience, shaped by real moments, and flexible enough to meet you wherever you are. These aren't rigid steps. They're invitations. To pause. To reflect. To move with more presence.

Framework in Motion: How the MOVING Method Evolves

The MOVING Method grows with you. Whether you're just beginning or evolving through a new chapter, the method meets you right where you are.

Letter	At the Start	In Transition	Moving Forward
M	Motivation—What's calling you to begin?	Mindset—What beliefs need tending?	Make Space—What needs room to grow?
O	Organization—Create structure.	Order—What brings calm and clarity?	Ownership—What are you choosing?
V	Vision—What do you want to feel?	Values—What keeps you aligned?	Voice—Say what's true for you.
I	Involvement—Who's with you?	Insight—What are you learning?	Intuition—What are you trusting?
N	Now—Focus on what's right in front.	Next—Anticipate the shift.	Navigation—Stay grounded in flow.
G	Grace—Be soft with yourself.	Growth—Change is unfolding.	Grounding—Celebrate the roots.

Unpack: From Transition to Transformation

- What patterns keep showing up in your life that might point to a skill, strength, or calling?

- When have you helped someone and realized afterward, "I'm really good at this?"

- What if the thing you've done quietly for years is actually your next move?

You don't need a business plan to begin. You just need to notice where your skills and someone's need consistently meet.

💬 *Moving Thought*

The MOVING Method didn't come from a master plan— it came from motion. From saying yes before I knew the outcome. From organizing one moment at a time until a framework revealed itself.

You don't have to wait until it all makes sense. You just have to start where you are. The clarity comes in the doing. The framework often lives in the very thing you've done quietly for years.

What if what you've already lived is the method?

CHAPTER 12:

Celebrate the Move

 Unpack: What Are You Moving Into?

Look at how you showed up.
Not just in the big moments—
but in the quiet ones.
The hard decisions.
The small shifts.
The days when it would've been easier to ignore the boxes.

You still made space.
You named your move.
You made a plan.
You questioned what to keep.
You let go of what was never yours to carry.
You asked for help.
You trusted your gut.
You moved.

Maybe you cried.
Maybe you changed your mind.
Maybe you paused.
All of it counts.

This is what growth looks like:
You didn't just move your things.
You met yourself.

 **Jevata-ism**

You don't need every answer. Just one next step.
The MOVING Method is ready whenever you are.

This isn't just about celebrating the finished product.
It's about celebrating you—
the way you showed up, shifted, chose again.

Every step counts—even the ones you didn't think were brave at the time.

Celebration is the rhythm.
The acknowledgment of the pause.
The toast to progress.
The moment you finally see what's been changing inside you all along.

✍ Journal with Me: Becoming

- What are you moving into now?

- Does your Move Name still fit?

- What are you proud of—not just for what got done, but for how you showed up?

Write a simple statement:

I am celebrating what I am moving into: _____

_____

Let this be your mantra.
Your mirror.
Your milestone.

Growth Through Celebration

You may be surprised by how much has shifted.
More importantly, this is your moment to claim progress, not perfection.

Recognize the small wins:
Making a phone call.
Sorting one drawer.
Saying no.
Saying yes.

Celebration is how you stay grounded.
It's how you keep going.
It's not about grand gestures—it's about creating a mantra
that says:
Yes, you did.
Yes, you can.
Yes, you will.

Because in the end, this move may not just be about
relocating.
It may be about finally retiring.
Moving out of your parents' house.
Changing careers.
Choosing yourself.
Letting go of something that once defined you.

The boxes are just the beginning.
However you name your move, let this pause honor both
where you've been—
and where you're headed next.

✖ TOOL #2 – *Name Your Move Worksheet*

Tools are part of celebration, too—
they remind you that progress is something you can see,
name, and return to.

When you pause to honor what you've accomplished—even
if it's just unpacking one room, donating one box, or making
one difficult decision—you give your nervous system a
chance to exhale.

You signal to yourself: *I'm safe. I'm progressing. I belong here.*

We don't just grow by checking things off a list—
we grow by noticing what it took to get here.

Celebration isn't extra.
It's essential.
It's self-care.

Celebrating the move means honoring the effort, not just the outcome.
It reminds us we don't have to wait until the home is "done" to start living in it—
we are already living through it, reshaping our spaces and ourselves, moment by moment.

📖 Nia's Journey: Celebrating Along the Way

The sun was beginning to set, casting a golden hue across Nia's freshly organized living room.
She had just finished unpacking the last box from her *Kitchen + Comfort* project—a section of her Move Plan she'd color-coded with orange for warmth and nourishment.

She sat on the edge of her new sofa, reached for her Move Plan binder, and flipped to the page labeled:
Milestone: Kitchen Complete → Reward: Favorite Wine + Music Night.

She smiled—surprised she'd remembered to follow through. So often she had skipped over her own achievements, racing to the next task without pause. But this time was different.
She went to the kitchen, pulled out a chilled bottle of her favorite rosé, lit the candle her best friend had given her, and opened the playlist she'd made the night she decided to move.

As the music filled the room and the wine warmed her chest, she didn't think about what was left to do.
She thought about how far she'd come.

Hundreds of tiny decisions—what to keep, what to let go, who to call, when to rest, how to trust herself again.
Each one a pebble on the path that led here: a soft, grounded space that reflected who she was becoming.

Her glass wasn't raised to mark the end—
it was lifted to honor the becoming.

And if she could pause and honor her own path, maybe you can, too.

This was growth: not an empty to-do list, but a full heart.
A space that echoed her values.
A moment of joy she had created—for herself, by herself.

She raised her glass quietly and whispered, "I'm proud of you."
And in that quiet moment, surrounded by music, intention, and the glow of soft light, she felt both her feet and her future planted firmly in place.

Unpack: Tune Into Your Space

You've been walking with Nia.
But really—
you've been walking with yourself.

Her questions were your questions.
Her fear. Your fear.
Her pause. Your pause.
Her courage. Your courage.

She wasn't a guide.
She was a reflection.

She moved because you did.

She let go because you did.

She arrived because you're arriving too.

You didn't just follow her story.

You wrote your own.

And that's the move that matters most.

 **Jevata-ism**
Progress isn't how fast you moved.
It's that you moved.

💬 *Moving Thought*

Celebration isn't about getting it perfect.
It's about recognizing who you became along the way.

Let every candle lit, every drawer cleared, every deep breath be proof:

You didn't just move.
You moved forward.
You moved in.

You moved into yourself.

You did that.

And that's enough.

Because in the end — just as we said in the beginning — moving is more than boxes — it is about you.

EPILOGUE
The Letter in the Box.

I opened a letter today.

Why today?
Because I just finished *Moving in Place.*

I told myself to write this before I started—
so I'd remember how it felt to be standing at the edge,
not knowing if I could really do it.

It's been in the memory box where I keep my journals,
pushed to the back of a closet.
On top, in my handwriting: **To be opened when you arrive.**
I unfolded it.

To shift. To be in transition. To act. To become.

Jevata,

You have a title—*Moving in Place.*
You love it... but you're not sure it will work.
You're not even sure you'll keep it.

What if people don't get it?
What if it doesn't fit the book once you've written it?
What if it means something to you, but nothing to
anyone else?

Can I write a book about moving and keep me out of it?
The answer... probably not.
You've read other books about organizing.
Maybe you should model your book like theirs?
Would that make it "right"?

What makes you an expert?
Can you really write a best-selling book about moving?

You keep reminding yourself:
I am a move manager, not a life coach.
This book can't drift too far from what I actually do.
It has to help people move — not just "feel inspired" to move.

One friend told you, "You have control of what you show people."
Another said, "You have to be okay being vulnerable —
I know you'll wrestle with this."

They're both right. And you know it.
You don't have the whole picture.
You don't even have all the chapters.

But you have something—three words you can't stop coming back to:
Grace. Clarity. Authenticity.

Somewhere between doubt and determination, the words began to take shape:

Moving – To shift. To be in transition. To act. To become.
In – To be within something. To belong. To stay present.
Place – A location. A role. A way of being.

Together, these words are your way forward.
This is how you'll explain it to yourself first, and then to everyone else.

And if you forget everything else, remember this:

May you make peace with what you've carried, and release what no longer fits.
May your home be a mirror of your values and a container for your joy.
May your new space reflect your true self—boldly, tenderly, without apology.
And may every move – physical or otherwise – bring you closer to the life you desire and deserve.

You are not standing still.
You are moving in place.

And that's more than enough.

With grace,
You.

The Moving Toolkit

The MOVING Method™ was designed to help you navigate your move with more than just checklists.

It's how I work with clients. It's how I make sense of the chaos. It's how I guide people through overwhelm toward clarity. You've seen these tools throughout the book, woven into the stories and steps. But if you are starting here, that works too. Each one stands on its own. I use them whenever.

This toolkit holds the same tools I've used with real people, in real homes, through real transitions. They're flexible. And they're here for you — whether you're just beginning or already deep in the process.

This section brings the method to life — in your hands, your home, and your rhythm. There's no one right way to use it. No pressure to finish it all. No shame in coming back later. These tools exist to support your Move.

As a reminder: structure is not a constraint — it's a form of care.

You'll first find a moving tool reference guide — a one-page map of all the tools, and where they appear in the book. From there, each tool is presented with clear instructions, reflection prompts, and space to plan or track your progress.

To help you navigate the sections and tools throughout the book visually, we've included an **Emoji Key** — a quick guide to the symbols used throughout the book. These icons are here to make the method easier to follow, whether you're pausing for reflection, jotting a journal note, or applying a tip in real time.

When used together, these tools help you build your Move Plan — a clear, grounded framework that reflects your goals, values, and next steps.

What is The MOVING Method™?

The MOVING Method is a practical, flexible framework for navigating any life transition—whether you're clearing a loved one's home, starting over, or reclaiming space for yourself. It offers both **emotional grounding** and **tactical structure**, helping you move forward with **clarity, presence, and self-trust**.

Each letter represents a core focus area that shows up in every kind of move. The method supports decision-making, organization, and momentum—without forcing a one-size-fits-all path.

This is your compass. It won't just tell you what to do— It will help you remember **why it matters**.

MOVING Method™ Framework Overview

Letter	Themes	Focus	Guiding Questions
M	Motivation, Mindset, Make Space	Name your move, map your why, and clear space—physically and emotionally—for what's next.	Why am I moving? What needs to shift or open?
O	Ownership, Organization, Order	Step into the lead, own your story, and structure the support you need.	What's real right now? What needs structure?
V	Vision, Values, Voice	Define what matters most—and let your next chapter reflect it clearly.	What do I want? What matters most?
I	Involvement, Intuition, Insight	Trust your gut, ask for help, and stay connected to your inner knowing.	Who's with me? What do I know deep down?
N	Navigation, Now, Next	Take it one step at a time. Set your course. Move from now to next with clarity.	What's the next right step?
G	Growth, Grace, Grounding	Reflect on your journey. Release what no longer fits. Carry forward only what honors who you're becoming.	How am I becoming? How do I reflect and stay rooted?

MOVING Toolkit Reference Guide

This chart gives you a quick overview of all ten tactical tools featured in *Moving in Place*. Each one connects directly to a letter in the MOVING Method™ and supports a key moment in your transition. Use this guide to locate the right tool for where you are—emotionally, practically, or both.

You don't have to use every tool in order. Let your current needs guide you. Whether you're making your first move or your fifth, this framework is here to walk with you—not ahead of you.

MOVING Toolkit Reference Guide

Tool #	Title	Subtitle	MOVING Letter	Chapter Reference
1	Moving Method Tracker	A check-in tool to support your process	N / I	Introduction, Chapter 5
2	Move Type and Vision Statement	Define the purpose and emotion behind your move	M / V	Chapters 1, 5
3	Name Your Move Worksheet	Give your journey a name and emotional identity	M / G	Chapters 2, 5, 12
4	Move Readiness Check-In	A self-check before the plan begins	M	Chapters 3, 5
5	Move Plan Template	Turn your reflections into action	ALL	Chapters 4, 5, 9
6	Value Mapping	Map your responsibilities and emotional energy	O / V	Chapters 5, 10
7	4-Box Sorting	An efficient way to sort by use, need, and value	O / V	Chapter 5, 9
8	Legacy List Worksheet	Identify what matters before deciding what stays	V	Chapter 5, 7
9	Moving Circle Worksheet	Know who's supporting your move — and how	I	Chapters 5, 9
10	Letter to Your Future Self	Write from today's clarity to tomorrow's courage	G / V	Chapters 5, 10, 12

How to Use the Icons in This Book

Throughout *Moving in Place*, you'll see visual icons that signal different kinds of reflection, action, and support. These aren't just decorative—they're cues to help you engage more deeply with the material in the way that best supports you. Use this key to understand what each symbol means and when to pause, journal, or simply take a breath.

Emoji Key—Reflection Features Used Throughout the Book

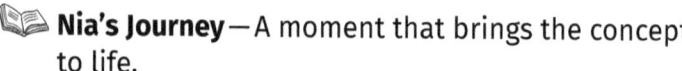 **Nia's Journey**—A moment that brings the concept to life.

✗ **MOVING Tools**—Offers practical frameworks, checklists, prompts, and templates you can put to use right away for clarity and momentum.

📦 **Unpack**—Creates space to reflect on what you're carrying—physically and emotionally—and what you're ready to release.

✍️ **Journal With Me**—Invites deeper exploration through writing or quiet thought, helping you name what matters and what's next.

💬 *Moving Thought*—Shares short truths to keep as mantras and intentions—quick reminders to ground and guide you.

✪ **Jevata-isms**—Delivers small truths—nudges, whispers, and grounding breaths drawn from my own lived experience with moving and change.

TOOL 1: **MOVING Method**™ **Tracker**

A space to pause, notice, and return to what matters.

Instructions:

This page isn't a checklist—it's a compass. Use it whenever you need to reflect on where you are, what's shifting, and what needs your attention next.

Each section of the MOVING Method™ represents a part of your journey. Write down what you're experiencing, questioning, or working on under each letter. There's no right order, and no rush. Let this check-in be a place of honesty, clarity, and care.

You can:

- Use this at the start, middle, or end of your move
- Write freely—thoughts, emotions, tasks, insights
- Return to this page as often as you need

Think of it as a moment to re-center before your next move.

Your MOVING Method™ Tracker

Letter	What's Happening for Me Here? (Write freely—thoughts, feelings, actions, needs)
M	
O	
V	
I	
N	
G	

TOOL 2:
Move Type and Vision Statement Worksheet

*A moment to check in before anything changes
on the outside.*

Step 1: Choose Your Move Type

Every move has a shape. Some are quiet. Some are chaotic. Some are about grief, others about growth.

Before you dive into deeper reflection, take a moment to name what kind of move you're making. These Move Types aren't boxes to fit into—they're guideposts to help you understand your season. If none feel quite right, feel free to write in your own.

☐ **Legacy Move**—Sorting through a lifetime of belongings, often after a loss

☐ **Reclaim Move**—Taking back your space, energy, or story

☐ **Merge & Move**—Blending lives, styles, or generations

☐ **Fresh Start Move**—Letting go of the past to begin again

☐ **Opportunity Move**—Saying yes to a new job, city, or chapter

☐ **Method Move**—Using the MOVING Method™ to create clarity, even if you're not physically moving

☐ **Other:**_____
Describe your move in your own words.

Step 2: Reflect + Write

This is your chance to define how you want to feel, what you're releasing, and what values will guide your next chapter.

• I am moving because:

• What does this move mean to me?

• This move will allow me to:

• What do I want my next space to feel like?

• What personal values do I want my space to reflect?

Step 3: Write Your Vision Statement

Now, pull it all together in your own words.

This is the beginning of your Move Vision Statement—something to return to whenever the process feels messy or hard.

Need a starting point? Try this sentence structure:

"I am moving because _____ **I want to feel**

_____ **This move will allow me to** _____ **"**

TOOL 3: **Name Your Move Worksheet**

A tool to give your transition an identity you can return to.

What It's For

Every move tells a story. And every story deserves a name.

Once you've written your Move Vision Statement and picked a Move Type, take a moment to title this chapter of your life. Naming your move gives it shape, emotional focus, and a sense of purpose you can return to again and again.

But moves change—and so can your title.

This tool isn't just for the beginning. If you're entering a new phase—unpacking, reclaiming, or starting fresh—you may want to rename your move to reflect your growth.

Examples

- Making Room for Me → Living Fully in My Space
- The Great Unbecoming → Becoming Who I Am
- Letting Go → Leaning In
- Not My Mom's House → My House Now

Your Move Name: _____

My Move Is Called: _____

_____

_____

_____

✍️ Journal with Me: Why This Name?

• What season or shift does this name represent?

• How does it reflect your mindset or intentions right now?

• If this is a renaming, what changed — and why does that matter?

• What do you want this title to remind you of moving forward?

Take a few moments to reflect. You're not just naming a move. You're naming what matters now.

Use This in Your Move Plan When you build your full Move Plan (in Chapter 5), this move name becomes your anchor. It will appear at the very top — reminding you why you began, who you're becoming, and what this move really means.

TOOL 4: **Move Readiness Check-In**

This tool lives in Chapter 3 and is meant to be a mirror, not a test.

Use it any time you feel unsure, stuck, overwhelmed, or emotionally tangled in the process.

This self-assessment helps you:
• Check in with your mindset and energy
• Name what might be holding you back
• Ground yourself before making major decisions
• Clarify whether you're reacting, avoiding, or truly ready to begin

This Is Your Pause Before the Plan

Whether you revisit it before building your Move Plan — or mid-move when things feel chaotic — this tool helps you slow down, get honest, and move forward with intention.

You don't have to be fearless. Just willing.

How to Use This in Your Move Plan In your Move Plan (Chapter 5), there's a section titled "Current Situation." This is where your insights from the Move Readiness Check-In belong. Write down what feels clear, what feels heavy, and what feels uncertain.

Think of it as your starting line — not where you want to go, but where you are right now.

The more honest you are here, the more aligned your next steps will be.

Where to Find the Full Tool The complete Move Readiness Check-In and interpretation are printed in full in Chapter 3. This is the only tool fully embedded in the main book, designed to be used in real time during your reflection process.

✕ TOOL 5: **Move Plan Template**

Your Move Plan: How and Why to Use It

Your Move Plan is more than a checklist—it's your personal guide through one of life's most demanding transitions.

Moves can feel chaotic because so many decisions, deadlines, and emotions compete for your attention. A Move Plan brings order to that chaos. It helps you:

- See the whole picture—so you're not just reacting to the next urgent thing.

- Make intentional choices—about what to do, when, and why.

- Stay grounded in your "why"—so your decisions align with your vision and values.

- Track your progress—so you can celebrate wins and adjust as needed.

Think of it as both your anchor and your map—evolving with you from the moment you name your move, through the packing tape stage, and into the life you're building on the other side.

Tips for Getting Started

- Start where you are—fill in what you know now and add as you gain clarity.

- Work in sections—complete one part at a time if you're feeling overwhelmed.

- Keep it visible—place it somewhere you'll see and use often.

- Update regularly—check in weekly (or more) to adjust timelines, roles, and tasks.

- Pair it with your Toolkit—for tools and deeper guidance linked to each section.

- Give yourself grace—this is a guide, not a scorecard; progress comes in waves.

Move Name

Purpose:

Your Move Name gives identity and intention to this transition. It's more than a label—it's a reminder of why you're doing this and where you're headed.

Instructions:

Choose a name that feels personal and motivating. It could be literal ("The Elm Street Downsizing"), emotional ("The Fresh Start Move"), or symbolic ("Project Lightness").

Write it here, and let it serve as your rallying cry for the weeks ahead.

Your Move Name: _____

Project Summary

Purpose:

Your Project Summary is the snapshot of your move—the "at a glance" story of what's happening. It keeps the big picture front and center so anyone reading it understands the scope and purpose of your transition.

Instructions:

Write 3–5 sentences that capture the essentials:

- **What's changing**—describe the core move (selling, buying, downsizing, relocating, etc.).

- **Why it's happening**—note the main reason or motivation.

- **Key timing**—include your anticipated move date or major milestones.

This is not your full plan—it's your elevator pitch for the move, a quick reference that keeps you focused and helps you explain your situation to others.

Your Project Summary:

_____

_____

_____

Move Type

Purpose:

Your Move Type describes your current situation and serves as a lens for decision-making. It helps you identify which tools, strategies, and support will serve you best.

Instructions:

Select the Move Type that fits best right now—your situation may shift, and that's okay. If it changes, update this section to reflect where you are.

- **Legacy** – Clearing and transitioning after the passing of a loved one.

- **Reclaim** – Taking back your space or life after a major shift or challenge.

- **Merge & Move** – Combining households or blending belongings.

- **Fresh Start** – Relocating to begin a new chapter with intention.

- **Opportunity** – Moving for a specific opening, job, or experience.

- **Method** – A self-led move using the MOVING Method™ tools independently.

Your Move Type: _____

Current Situation

Purpose:

Capture a clear, honest snapshot of where you're starting—your "before picture." This isn't about judgment; it's about awareness.

Instructions:

Describe your living situation right now, including:

- Size and layout of your space

- Amount and type of belongings you have

- Problem areas (e.g., overcrowded storage, rooms you avoid)

- Emotional climate (how you feel in your space right now)

- Any recent changes affecting your move (loss, job change, family shift, etc.)

Why It Matters:

A clear starting point helps you make better decisions about what to keep, let go of, or change—and gives you a baseline to see how far you've come.

Current Situation:

_____

_____

_____

Goal of the Move

Purpose:

Define your primary objective so every decision during the move supports this outcome.

Instructions:

Write 1–3 clear statements describing what you want to accomplish. Keep them specific and measurable where possible. Think about the finish line—what needs to be true for you to feel the move was worth it?

Examples:

- Downsize from a 3-bedroom home to a 1-bedroom apartment near downtown.

- Relocate to be closer to family while reducing commute time.

- Clear my parents' estate and prepare the property for sale.

Tip:

This is the practical anchor of your Move Plan. Unlike your Vision + Success Statement (which reflects how you want to feel), this section focuses on concrete results.

Goal(s):

_____

_____

_____

Vision + Success Statement

Purpose:

Your vision is the big picture—the why behind your move. Your success statement is how you'll know you've achieved it. Together, they give you a destination and a way to measure progress.

Instructions:

1. **Start with your vision**—Imagine your life and space after the move. What does it look like? How does it feel? Who is there with you?

2. **Define success**—Write in your own terms what will tell you the move was successful. This is about creating a life and space that reflect your values.

3. **Keep it specific but inspiring**—It should be something you can revisit when things feel hard.

4. **Write in present tense**—As if it's already real.

Example:

"I wake up in a space that feels calm and uncluttered. My home reflects my personality, and I have room to host family without feeling overwhelmed."

Tip:

Your vision should inspire you. Your success statement should ground you.

Vision:

_____

_____

_____

_____

_____

Success Statement:

_____

_____

_____

_____

_____

_____

Timeline + Key Milestones

Purpose:

A clear timeline keeps your move on track. Milestones help you see progress, spot delays early, and reduce last-minute stress.

Instructions:

1. **Choose your move date** — or your target completion date if the move is gradual.

2. **Work backward** — Identify major phases (decluttering, packing, moving day, unpacking) and set realistic dates for each.

3. **Add checkpoints** — These are the smaller wins along the way (e.g., "kitchen packed," "lease signed," "donation drop-off complete").

4. **Keep it flexible** — Life happens; adjust when needed, but stay mindful of the overall goal.

5. **Highlight the non-negotiables**—These are deadlines that can't be missed, like closing dates or travel arrangements.

Example:

- Aug. 15 – Finish decluttering bedroom

- Sept. 1 – Movers booked and confirmed

- Sept. 15 – Begin packing non-essentials

- Oct. 1 – Move day

- Oct 15 – Unpack essentials and set up living room

Tip:

Don't overfill your timeline. Leave room for unexpected delays and rest days.

Target Move Date: _____

Milestones:

1. _____

2. _____

3. _____

People Involved + Roles

Purpose:

Every move involves people—whether they're helping hands, decision-makers, or professionals you've hired. Defining who's involved and what they're responsible for keeps communication clear and prevents last-minute confusion.

Instructions:

1. **List everyone involved**—Include friends, family, contractors, movers, realtors, or anyone playing a role in your move. Add contact information if available.

2. **Clarify roles**—Be specific. "Help pack kitchen" is clearer than "help pack."

3. **Share expectations**—Make sure each person knows their role, timeline, and how to contact you.

4. **Identify key decision-makers**—Note who can approve expenses, sign paperwork, or make final calls.

5. **Be honest about your role in the move, too**— what responsibilities you're keeping on your plate.

Example:

- Maria (sister)–Assist with decluttering and donation drop-offs on weekends

- John's Moving Co.–Handle loading, transportation, and unloading on move day

- Alex (realtor)–Coordinate closing and final walk-through

Tip:

This section can also help you spot gaps—if no one is handling a key task, assign it before it becomes urgent.

People Involved + Their Roles:

1. _____

2. _____

3. _____

4. _____

Key Projects +Tasks

Purpose:

Every move is made up of smaller projects and tasks. Breaking your move into clear, manageable pieces helps you see progress and stay on track.

Instructions:

1. **List your major projects first**—Examples: "Declutter the garage," "Schedule movers," "Set up utilities."

2. **Add supporting tasks**—Under each project, write the smaller steps needed to complete it.

3. **Prioritize**—Mark what needs to be done first, and what can wait.

4. **Assign responsibilities and deadlines**—Use realistic dates to prevent last-minute stress.

5. **Review often** — Update this list as tasks are completed or new ones come up.

Example:

- Project: Declutter Kitchen

  - Sort pantry items

  - Donate unused small appliances

  - Pack remaining items in labeled boxes

Tip:

This section becomes your go-to action plan. Check it before starting each day to keep momentum going.

Key Projects + Tasks:

1. _____

2. _____

3. _____

4. _____

Self-Care + Stress Management

Purpose:

A successful move isn't just about getting boxes from one place to another — it's also about protecting your energy, focus, and well-being along the way. This section helps you plan for rest, resilience, and balance so you can arrive at your new space feeling grounded.

Instructions:

1. **Identify what nourishes you** — Think about the activities, people, or routines that help you recharge.

2 **Plan for breaks** — Moving is physically and emotionally demanding; schedule downtime like you would any other task.

3. **Name your stress signals** — Recognizing when you're feeling overwhelmed helps you take action sooner.

4. **Choose support systems** — List people, services, or resources you can call on when things feel heavy.

5. **Keep it realistic** — Self-care can be as simple as staying hydrated, getting enough sleep, or stepping outside for fresh air.

Example:

- Nourishing Activity: Morning walk before packing begins

- Stress Signal: Feeling irritable or rushing decisions

- Support System: Call a friend for a 10-minute reset

Tip:

Protecting your well-being is part of the move itself—it's how you make sure you can keep going until the very end.

Self-Care + Stress Management Plan:

- Nourishing Activities: _____

- Stress Signals: _____

- Support Systems: _____

- Other Notes: _____

    _____

    _____

Want to complete this digitally or print it out? Scan the QR code or visit www.projectmovelv.com/moveplan to download your template.

✗ TOOL 6: **Value Mapping**

Using Your Values to Make Confident Decisions

Your values are the invisible threads running through every decision you'll make in this move. When you get stuck—emotionally, logistically, or practically—your values become your compass.

This exercise helps you name and define the values that matter most right now, so they can shape how you move, what you keep, how you design your space, and the pace you take.

Step 1: Choose Your Top 3–5 Core Values

Scan the list below and highlight any values that stand out. Then narrow it down to the 3–5 that feel most essential for this move. Feel free to add your own to the list.

Sample Values:

• Adventure	• Gratitude	• Purpose
• Authenticity	• Growth	• Security
• Balance	• Honesty	• Self-Love
• Beauty	• Integrity	• Simplicity
• Calm	• Joy	• Spirituality
• Clarity	• Justice	• Strength
• Community	• Kindness	• Stability
• Creativity	• Legacy	• Trust
• Family	• Love	• Wellness
• Freedom	• Peace	

My Top Values:

1. _____

2. _____

3. _____

4. _____

5. _____

**Step 2: Define What They Mean to You —
and Why They Matter**

For each value, write a short sentence describing what it
means in the context of your move.

Example: "Clarity means having fewer distractions in my
space and a plan I can follow."

1. _____

2. _____

3. _____

4. _____

5. _____

Step 3: Apply Your Values to Your Move Plan

Let your values guide decisions about:

- What to keep or let go of
- How to design your new space
- What kind of support you need
- The pace that feels right for you

Use This in Your Plan: Keep this list visible. Revisit it when you feel overwhelmed, stuck, or unsure. Let your values shape not just how your home looks—but how it feels.

This is your compass. Let it guide the way you move.

Bonus: Vision Journaling with Values

Want to go deeper? Pair your values with images, sketches, or inspiration that capture how you want your life and space to feel.

Ideas to try:

- Clip images from magazines or print photos that represent your values.

- Create a mini vision board that shows what "joy," "freedom," or "clarity" looks like to you.

- Journal a page for each value with textures, colors, or spaces that reflect what you're moving toward.

This is about more than decorating—it's about seeing your values *in action.*

✂ TOOL 7: **4-Box Sorting Method**

A streamlined way to make clear, confident decisions— room by room.

When you're moving, you're not just decluttering a drawer— you're often staring down an entire house of stuff. This method offers an efficient, values-in-action approach to move through spaces without getting emotionally overwhelmed.

The 4-Box Method helps you make decisions based on use, need, and value—giving your brain something structured to lean on when your emotions feel loud. It turns your core values into practical filters, helping you act on your Move Vision Statement with every choice you make.

It's not just about what to toss. It's about what to carry forward, honor, or release with clarity.

How to Use the 4 Boxes

Sort your items into four categories as you move through each space. This method helps you move logically and quickly without ignoring what matters:

Box Name	Purpose	Emotional Cue
Keep	Items you use, need, or deeply value	"This still belongs with me."
Rehome	Items to pass on with intention (to people or places)	"Someone else can use or love this."
Release	Items that no longer serve your space or story	"I release this with clarity."
Hold	Items you're not ready to decide on yet	"I need more time or support around this."

Tips for Real-Life Use:

- Use bins, bags, or sticky notes to label boxes.
- Re-evaluate the "Hold" box often to keep the pile small.
- Don't overthink—lead with logic first, then review for emotion later.
- Keep your core values in mind. Ask: *Does this support the way I want to live next?*

Sorting this way isn't about perfection—it's about momentum. It gives you a way to move forward, one decision at a time.

✗ TOOL 8: **Legacy List Worksheet**

What do I keep when everything holds meaning?

When you're surrounded by items filled with memory, it can feel impossible to know what to keep. The Legacy List helps shift the question from "Should I keep this?" to "Does this reflect my values—or who I'm becoming?"

This tool is rooted in emotion and guided by clarity. It's especially helpful when you're afraid of making a mistake or losing something important. Many people begin the process wanting to keep everything—just in case. The Legacy List creates space for thoughtful choices.

It invites you to ask: What types of things would feel devastating to lose? What carries family meaning? What has personal or practical significance? This list becomes a grounding reference as you move through your space.

How to Use the Legacy List

1. Name your core values. (Examples: connection, creativity, service, joy, beauty.)

2. List 5–10 items you're unsure about keeping or want to ensure are preserved. These could be:

- Photos or family albums
- Letters or journals
- Important papers or legal documents
- Jewelry or heirlooms
- Furniture with family history
- Clothing that carries a memory

Anything that stirs emotion or hesitation belongs on this list.

3. Reflect on each item by asking:
    - What memory or person is this connected to?
    - Does this item reflect one of my core values?
    - Does keeping it bring me joy, guilt, or obligation?
    - Is this something I want to pass on —
      or something I've outgrown?

4. Decide how to honor it:
    - Keep with purpose
    - Pass down with meaning
    - Document and release (e.g., take a photo, write a
      memory, then let it go)

Use This in Your Move Plan

Refer to your Legacy List when making decisions about what to keep, pass on, or prioritize during estate clearing, packing, or designing your next space.

You may want to begin this worksheet *before* or *during* the 4–Box Sorting process, especially if you're sorting through items with emotional or family significance.

You can also use it to:

- Identify items to protect or locate early
- Communicate clearly with family about what matters to you
- Capture emotional stories that may not have monetary value, but hold deep meaning

This tool helps ensure your Move Plan reflects more than logistics — it reflects your story.

Legacy List Template

Item Description	Memory or Meaning	Aligned Value	Keep / Release / Pass On	Notes
Ex. Grandma's teacup	Sunday tea together	Connection	Keep	Use for quiet mornings
Ex. Dad's toolbox	His way of fixing things	Practicality / Legacy	Pass On	Give to nephew
Ex. Old yearbooks	High school memories	None (no joy)	Release	Take photo of one page

This isn't about letting go. It's about choosing what carries your story forward—and ensuring what matters most doesn't get lost along the way.

✗ TOOL 9: **Moving Circle Worksheet**

You don't have to do this alone.

Your Moving Circle is the group of people who will help you through this move. It's more than who shows up on moving day—it's who you trust with the emotional, physical, and decision-making parts of this process.

This tool helps you clarify what kind of support you need, assign roles, and identify the people who can help carry both the boxes and the emotions.

Step 1: Define the Support You Need

Start with what you need—not who. This is about ownership. Ask yourself:

- What roles do I need help with?
- Why do I need them?
- When will I need them?
- What exactly do I want this person to do?

Use the table below to brainstorm the types of support that will lighten your load.

Category	Support Needed	Who Can Help
Emotional Support	Venting, calming	
Physical Labor	Lifting, packing	
Logistics	Scheduling, transport	
Decision Support	Sorting, letting go	

Step 2: Identify Your Circle

Now that you've named the roles, think about who in your life could realistically fill them.

- Who do you call when you're stuck?
- Who grounds you?
- Who can carry a box and a breakdown?

Name	Role / Support Type	Notes (Boundaries or Needs)

Use This in Your Move Plan

Include your Moving Circle in the "People + Roles" section of your Move Plan. Touch base with them early—clarity builds trust, and people want to help. You just have to invite them in.

This is about asking for support before you need it. The right people can help lighten the physical and emotional load—and give structure to your next steps.

✖ TOOL 10:

Letter to Your Future Self: A Lifeline to Hope

There's a moment in every move when the vision
gets blurry.
You're surrounded by tasks, emotions, decisions—
and you're just trying to make it through.

This letter isn't about getting it all right.
It's about naming your *why*, even when the finish line
feels far away.
It's about saying something true to yourself *before* fear,
fatigue, or forgetting steps in.

This letter is your **promise** to yourself.
Your **voice**, when you're too tired to speak.
Your **hope**, when you're not sure how it will all come together.

What This Letter Can Hold:

- Your reason for moving—even if it feels messy
- A vision for who you want to become
- A reminder of what you're letting go of
- A glimpse of what you hope to feel on the other side
- A moment of compassion from the version of you who dared to begin

How to Use This Tool:

Write the letter now—before the chaos, before the big
emotions drown out your why. Seal it in an envelope. Put it
in your "Open First" box.

You don't have to read it when you arrive.
You'll know when you need it.

From Me to You—And Me Again

When I said I was going to write a book, I was terrified.
The words didn't come.
I questioned whether I was enough.
But I kept showing up.
And I wrote letters to myself in the quiet—when I didn't yet believe I could do this.

Just like the times I asked someone to tell me I was doing good—because I couldn't see it yet.
This letter is for *that* version of you.
The one who is doing it afraid.
The one who's trying to hold it all together.
The one who needs permission to pause and feel.

Write what you hope the other side looks like.
Even if you can't see it yet.
Especially then.

You don't have to be brave every second.
You just have to be honest in this one.

About the Author

Jevata Crawford believes that moving is life — it's emotional, practical, and deeply human. As the founder of Project MOVE and the creator of the MOVING Method™, she helps people navigate life's transitions with clarity, care, and grace. Her approach blends structure with soul, guiding others to create spaces that reflect who they are and who they're becoming.

Before she ever wrote a method or packed a box, Jevata was telling stories — first to herself, then to others. Her background in sociology, her lived experience, and her work inside real homes shape every tool she shares. For her, storytelling is a way of making meaning, and moving is a way of remembering what matters.

She lives in the Lehigh Valley, Pa., where self-care looks like clean counters, quiet mornings, handwritten notes, and enough white space to breathe. Moving in Place is her invitation to move with intention — and to never underestimate the power of honoring your space, your story, and yourself.

www.ingramcontent.com/pod-product-compliance
Lightning Source LLC
Chambersburg PA
CBHW051204120626
46547CB00012B/1191